a painter & a poet

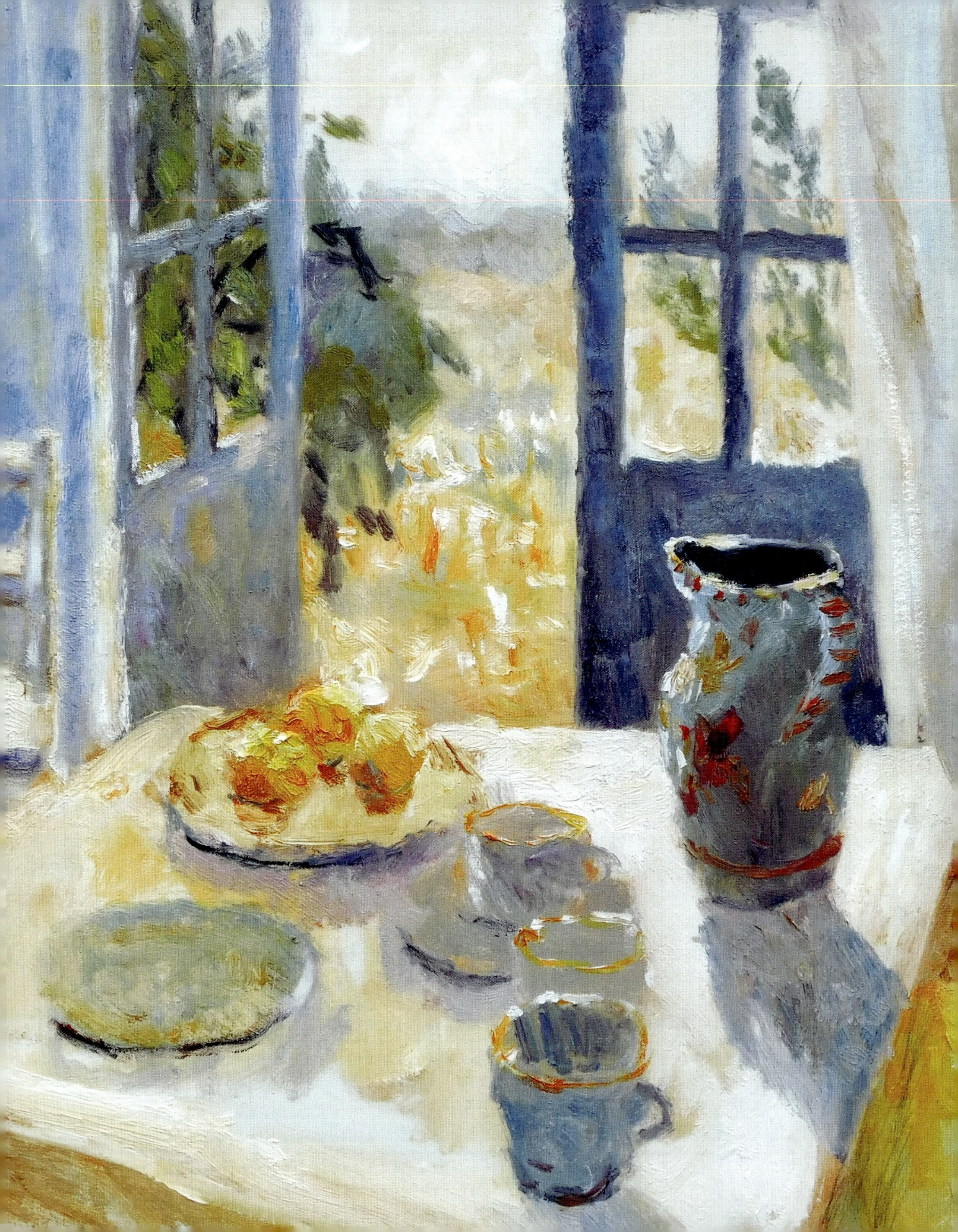

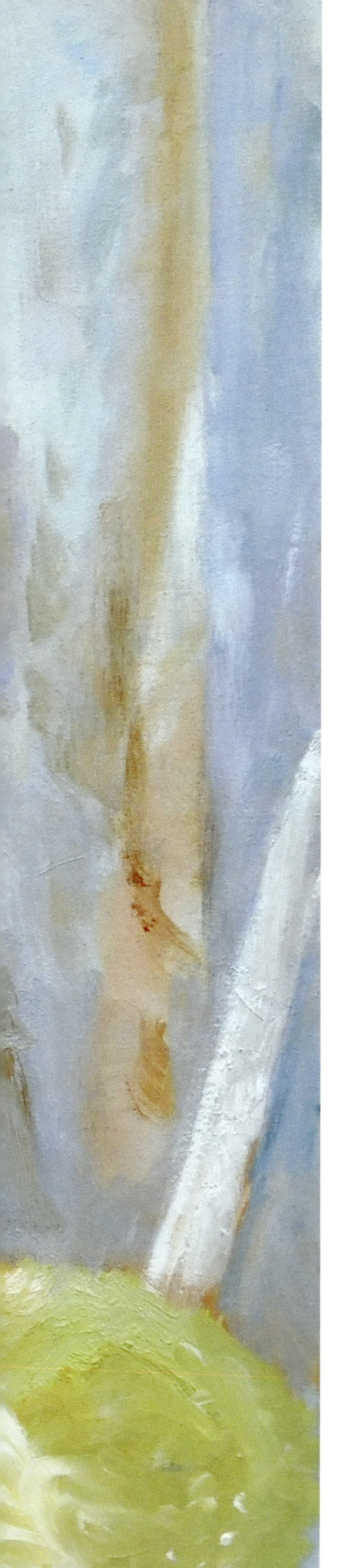

a painter & a poet

conversations in colour

Alice Mumford
& Sue Leigh

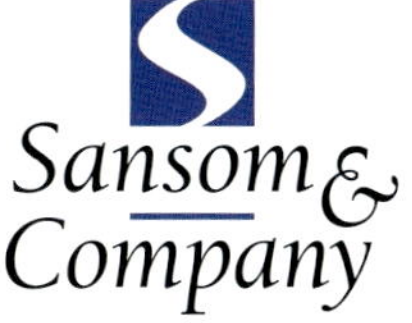

Sansom & Company

First published in 2023 by Sansom and Company,
a publishing imprint of Redcliffe Press Ltd.,
81G Pembroke Road, Bristol BS8 3EA
www.sansomandcompany.co.uk
info@sansomandcompany.co.uk

Published to coincide with the exhibition
'A Painter and a Poet: Conversations in Colour',
Alice Mumford with Sue Leigh, Belgrave St Ives,
9–30 September 2023

Paintings © Alice Mumford
Poems and text © Sue Leigh
Foreword © Kelly Grovier

ISBN 978-1-915670-06-9

British Library Cataloguing-in-Publication Data:
A catalogue record for this book is available from the
British Library. All rights reserved. Except for the purpose
of review, no part of this book may be reproduced, stored
in a retrieval system, or transmitted, in any form or by any
means, electronic, mechanical, photocopying, recording or
otherwise, without the prior permission of the publishers.

Commissioning editor: Paul Deaton
Copyediting: Ann Kay
Design and typesetting: E&P Design, Bath
Photography: David White (Alice Mumford, paintings);
Mark Leslie (Sue Leigh)
Printed and bound by Akcent Media

This book is made from Forest Stewardship Council®
certified paper. Sansom & Company is committed
to being an environmentally friendly publisher.

Front cover · *Summer Jasmine* [detail]
2021 · oil on canvas · 76 x 100 cm
Frontispiece · *French Doors Open, Late Autumn* [detail]
2022 · oil on canvas · 76 x 100 cm
Back cover: *Summer Picnic*
2022 · oil on canvas · 50 x 60 cm

contents

foreword

Kelly Grovier

Place a poem beside a painting and something almost mystical occurs. A space outside of space suddenly opens. In it, a new syntax and a new grammar – a language that is not verbal or visual, yet both – is formed: a conversation between strangers who share neither origin nor accent but a yearning for truth.

Place a poem by Sue Leigh beside a painting by Alice Mumford and the two begin to unlock possibilities in each other that would otherwise be inaccessible if either was encountered on its own. The words by Leigh do not ventriloquise Mumford's visions or seek to give them a voice they lack. Rather, Leigh's lyricism cooperates with Mumford's consciousness of colour to establish a place that never existed before. Together, the two enunciations – one echoing in the eye, the other in the ear – map a realm of luminous disquiet. 'When I think of your poems', Alice Mumford confesses to Sue Leigh in one of the fascinating conversations between painter and poet chronicled in this book, 'I think of colour … I am thinking of a colour and a place.'

Colour, it turns out, is the lucent lexicon in which the imaginations of these creators eloquently conspire. Take, for example, the unexpectedly edgy juxtaposition of Sue Leigh's deftly disorientating poem 'painting light' (p.70) and Alice Mumford's evocative oil-on-canvas *Summer Jasmine* (p.71). With every turn of Leigh's restless lines, Mumford's deceptively serene still life of an earthenware pitcher suspending a spray of jasmine in the shifting cerulean shadows of a quiet kitchen confesses a deep defiance of all things still:

> *summer jasmine is*
> *so white and starry*
> *it might be night, might be*
> *moonlight*

By glimpsing in the painter's noontide palette an elasticity of time and place – day that might be night, here that might be there – Leigh has penetrated to a truth she shares with Mumford: ours is a world of unfixable flux. Everything that is is something else. Jugs and pitchers, fashioned for the flow of fluid, slip into a strange stagnancy in which the decay of cut flowers is forever frozen. Chairs, poised for the heft of posture, cradle weightless silhouettes instead. Windows, glazed for the act of looking outward, glaze over into abstract opacity, hemming our eyes into carefully choreographed interiors that ache with absence.

Leigh too is drawn to the resplendence of residuals. 'I am interested in what we leave behind,' she tells Mumford, 'a standing stone, a piece of needlework, some tools.' To that list of toughly tender touchstones we could, perhaps, add the bright bric-a-brac of poems and paintings. These poems. These paintings. Somehow, against all cosmic odds, Leigh's and Mumford's lustrous expressions of wonder and bewilderment have found each other in life's blinding void to keep each other company. Oh, and us.

introduction

Sue Leigh

BEGINNINGS

I was looking for an image for the cover of my second collection of poems when I first encountered Alice's work. I was immediately drawn in to those intimate still lifes. A domestic interior, objects on a table, light falling from a window – Alice seemed to catch a fleeting moment of time. Looking at her paintings, I had a sense of both the presence and absence of human beings. It was as if someone had arranged the flowers in a jug and just left the room to let the cat out, fetch a book. I realised how Alice's paintings invite us to consider the beauty of our daily lives – a blustery sky, shadows, the simplicity of a blue jug. And what a blue! Alice's work is a festival of colour.

My book was to be called *Her Orchards*, and I wrote to Alice to see if she might allow me to use her painting, *Beech Leaves and Apple Blossom*, as the cover illustration. The painting – of blossom and the first new beech leaves casually placed in jugs in early morning light – conveyed a radiance and stillness that was almost other-worldly. And yet it was also concerned with the physical things of this world. My poems seemed to occupy a similar place, what I describe as 'neither here nor there'. When Alice told me she was happy for me to use her painting I was delighted.

And so began a friendship, discussions about our working lives as artists and the making of this book, which would accompany Alice's latest exhibition in St Ives. I would write a group of poems that would also appear in the book. We weren't sure how this would work, but we were intrigued. We were clear, however, that we wanted the paintings and poems to appear side by side, not as illustrations or explanations of each other, but quite simply illuminating one another. We hoped we might enrich the experience of both looking and reading.

SETTING OUT

Collaboration does not seem quite the right
word for what we were embarking on. We would
be working alongside each other rather than with
each other, although our discussions about art and
making informed our thinking. Would the poems
be quieter, the paintings more vibrant, insistent?
'Colour', as Pierre Bonnard said, 'can carry you
away.' Would the poems be more responsive?
(I was aware that there seemed to be more poems
responding to works of art than the other way
round.) We were excited to see what might happen.
We realised we were interested in similar things.
Each of us, in our own way, wanted to catch something of what the American poet Randall Jarrell
called 'the dailiness of life', the ordinary beauty
of it, but we were doing so in different media.
What were the limitations and possibilities
of each, we wondered. Can experience and our
sensory life only be fully expressed without words,
in art forms such as painting, music and dance?
But then, language is rich, the names of things
lovely. We had many ideas to think about.

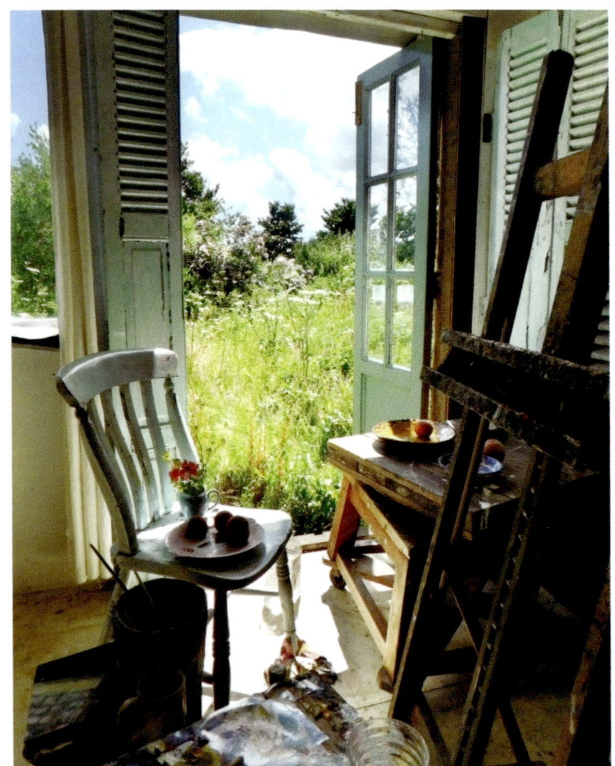

French doors at the studio, Polgrean Farm

AT POLGREAN

We decided that I would spend some days at
Alice's house in Polgrean. I already knew this
part of south-west Cornwall, with its deep lanes
and banks of ferns and red campion, its cliffs
noisy with gulls and choughs, as I had walked
the coastline some years before. (I had recorded
my journey in a notebook.) But to be at the farm,
with its wild garden and orchard, to spend time
in Alice's studio, offered a way into writing for
me. We walked to Prussia Cove, picked up shells
on Lelant beach, sat in the garden, talked. It was
early May, the huge beech was a tenderness of
leaves; the orchard was full of blossom and bees.

Later, I began to write the poems. They were
written not only in response to encountering
Alice's work but also as a way of capturing
the time I spent at Polgrean with her, and that
particular part of Cornwall. Place and landscape
seem so important to both of us. It was a very
freeing experience, as I allowed myself to write
whatever came to me. The paintings were starting
points in a way, but once I started writing other
ideas came, and I allowed myself to explore them
and see where they took me.

Alice continued to work on her own, sending me
photos of new paintings. I sent her poems. I think
we nourished each other. We both value solitude
but we had many conversations and shared ideas
about painting and poetry, process and place.

conversations

Sue Leigh [SL] *and Alice Mumford* [AM]

ROOMS, WITH A VIEW

[SL] How do we begin to make a picture, a poem? Where does it come from, that first impulse? I sometimes think it is like taking a step out into the dark.

[AM] I am unpredictable in my beginnings – and in most of my work. The one constant is that I only ever want to paint from life. I am not methodical, except when I am teaching. I think if you do everything systematically in the same way it doesn't feel like a natural response.

For me the business of sitting in front of something and responding to it is a sacred moment. Being, looking, contemplating raise profound questions about our existence. They encompass everything for me.

[SL] So many of your paintings are still lifes – a pink cloth on a table, a blue jug, summer flowers perhaps. Often there is a window or French doors, a landscape beyond (and we might return to this idea of bringing exterior and interior worlds together later). Do you begin by arranging, with an arrangement? Is that the way into painting for you?

[AM] I spend a long time setting up a still life, putting things in and then taking them out. At a certain point it becomes irresistible, the urge to paint. And I start. I remain immersed in painting until it has a completeness. Then I have to change gear, take the painting away from the subject, consider all options and make small adjustments, over many months.

[SL] Tracey Emin finds a blank canvas intimidating; she likes to draw first. Is this something you can relate to?

[AM] I may begin by putting blocks of colour next to each other without having thought about the structure of the painting (which comes later). At other times I find that drawing is a hugely meditative and instructive process. (I don't like pencils – the sharp point makes my brain go into writing mode, a different pathway. I only use the side of my pencil.)

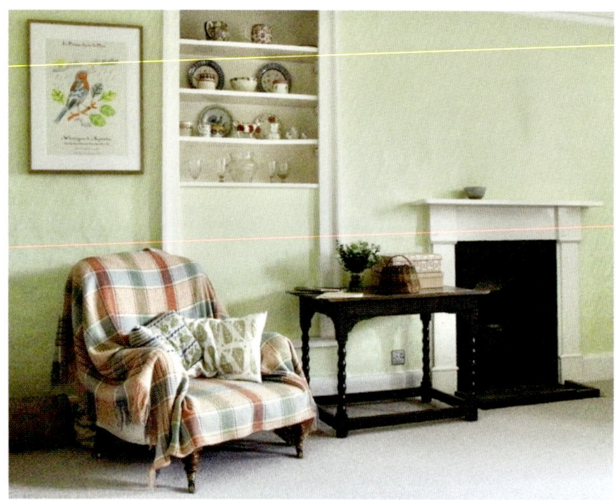

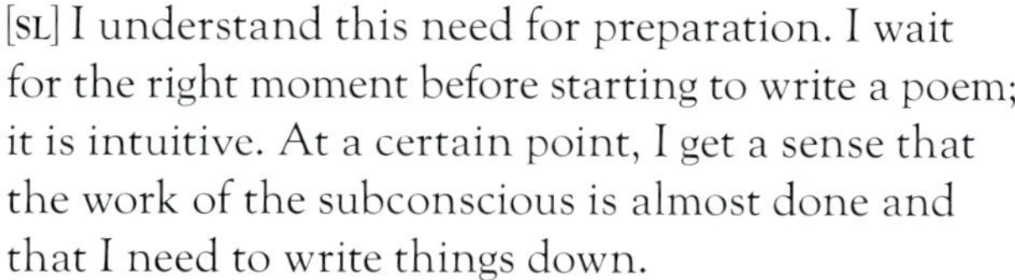

Sue's room, a quiet corner

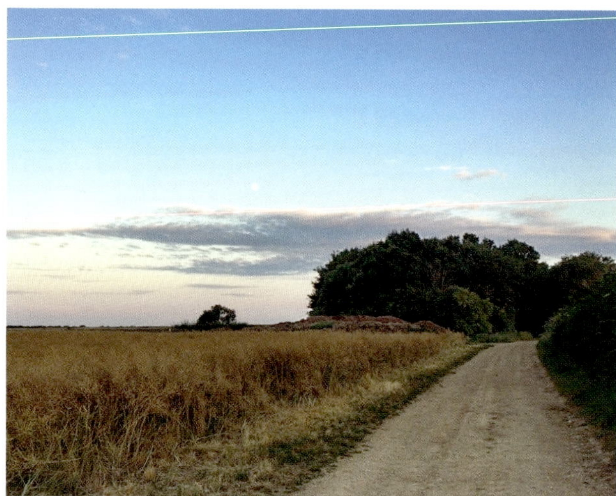

An evening walk, late summer

[SL] I understand this need for preparation. I wait for the right moment before starting to write a poem; it is intuitive. At a certain point, I get a sense that the work of the subconscious is almost done and that I need to write things down.

Rituals are important to me too. I spend much time walking. This is often where poems begin (it has something to do with rhythm, I think). Outside, there is a sense of lightness; the mind quietens, you can listen. You look at the sky; you inhabit weather. You move through the living world – a world of plants, creatures. You feel part of it.

I write in my notebook every day. I started this practice some years ago and I can't imagine ever not doing it. (I love the physical act of writing; I think this connection to the body is important.) I write down things I want to remember – the look of the landscape when I wake, redwings flying, something I heard on the radio, the remnants of a dream. Sometimes these notes may be the beginnings of a poem. (My working notebook, where I write poems, is another matter: it is very messy.)

I cannot say where poems come from, though, except from noticing, paying attention, a kind of intense listening. I love the mystery that surrounds their making. A line often leads me and I trust its sound. It is difficult to talk about process. In the end there are the poems and they must speak for themselves. And of course it is all provisional. There are times of writing and there are fallow periods. But I have learnt that these times of fallow

are as important as the writing itself. It has taken me a while to understand this.

[AM] I am interested that you mention the physical experience of writing (and this is true of many creative activities). We hold so many things in our body. If I have had a break, I have to limber up before painting, get my body to remember. And I understand about fallow. I have begun to love the winter, a time for recharging the batteries, laying down, collecting. Sometimes I wonder what it would be like if I never painted again. It would be like being told I would never see a friend again. I would miss the conversation – with myself, with my mother, a close confidante, the past, dead artists.

[SL] So you see painting as a conversation. I don't think I am aware of anyone else when I write. I am trying to get to a kind of truth, not a literal truth, an imaginative truth. In that dance with language I may get a little closer to it.

I am still thinking about how work happens. Virginia Woolf wrote in her diary that she had 'netted that great fin in the waste of water' after finishing *The Waves*. Most of the work is out of sight, there is just a glimpse of something. It is so much to do with time, isn't it? And patience. We have to judge the moment to begin.

[AM] We need to allow the chaos, not to overwork or attempt to pin things down. There should be imaginative space for the viewer. So the viewer

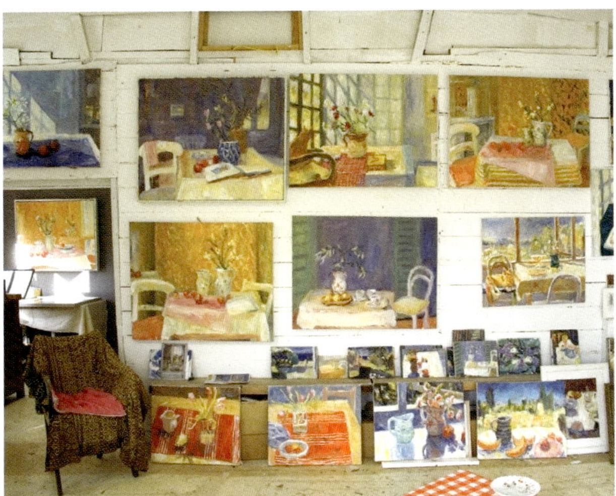

The studio at Polgrean Farm

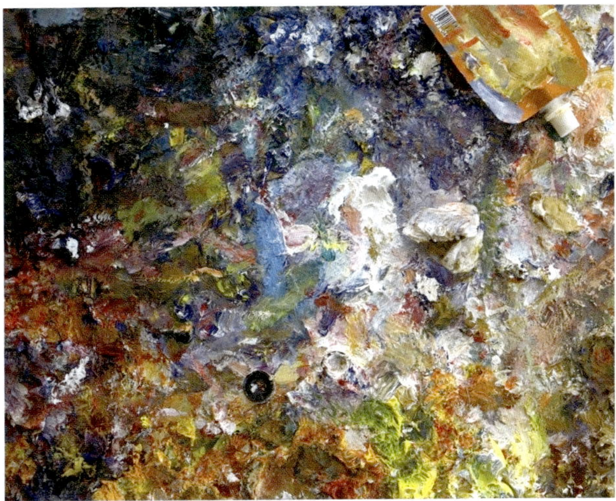

Alice's palette (and sun tan cream)

becomes a participant. I find definition difficult; I think that things that are just out of reach are more comprehensible.

[SL] And would you say you look for a subject, or does it find you? I go about my life and something lights up – it might be something I have read or seen or felt or remembered – and I know I will write a poem about it.

[AM] My subject is looking for a resonance within a room and the objects. Finding the objects can be problematic. I might see something and connect to it because of its shape, colour or scale. I then put it in a painting and it just doesn't work. When it does, it is as if I get inside the object. I was given a commission by the daughter of a potter based in St Ives. When I painted the pots it was a very different experience from just looking at them. I felt the handling of the clay and the reverence the potter had for the process of glazing.

Sometimes I paint with someone in mind; they are in my periphery vision. I think what I am probably looking for is a combination of all these things.

[SL] It is odd to use the word 'subject' in relation to a poem, as what a poem says cannot be said in any other way. I think of a poem as a little research project into one's relationship with the world. I return to ideas I want to explore – the deep past, questions of how we might live, how we might respond creatively to being alive. I write about the natural

world from a place of reverence but also concern. And, yes, I write about objects as they enable me to imagine another life, another time. I am interested in what we leave behind – a standing stone, a piece of needlework, some tools.

But I also want to be receptive to what might happen. I am sure artists need to approach things with that kind of openness and curiosity. Being with you, talking with you, I understand that even more now.

TELLING COLOUR

[SL] We work in different media. I wonder if we might share our experiences of working in the ways we do. I am interested in how you use colour, how you paint light. And also the places where we work.

[AM] Colour is something that stands almost as a quest in itself. I learnt so much about colour from Winifred Nicholson, in that you have to abandon just about everything to understand how colour works. It is interesting what she says about the way colour interacts with colour.

[SL] I read that she went out to pick a bunch of yellow flowers and her bunch would not 'tell yellow'. When she added two magenta everlasting peas, 'all my yellows broke into luminosity'. She also talked about the way colour takes you to a kind of territory of the human spirit.

[AM] Yes, colour has an emotional effect on us. We have our own inner libraries of colour; it is the layering of experience. (This is not the same with tone, the relative lightness or darkness of a colour.) With students, I often use Winifred Nicholson's colour scales (charts she devised to illustrate her very personal colour theories). Colour is experienced and re-experienced and layered in our memory.

[SL] And I am intrigued by how you paint light. Is it through using colour?

[AM] Yes. You can also use tone, but as I mentioned earlier colour connects to us emotionally in a different way. Often it will be a tussle between colour and tone, trying to get them to work together.

When I think of your poems I think of colour. I don't remember the words, I just respond to the visual impact. I am thinking of a colour and a place.

[SL] Colour and place are important to both of us but when I was writing the poems for this book I was thinking a great deal about colour. And I wonder about composition, how this works for you.

[AM] I have to try and avoid repeating the same compositions that don't work, for example splitting the canvas into two or putting something right in the middle of the canvas. I seem to be drawn to them like a moth to a flame. It is a conscious effort. I learn from Matisse. He would often have a large object at the bottom of the canvas. It acts like a diving board that you can jump off and enter the painting. I seek something with that in mind. And I have to improve my sense of scale. I remember some advice I was given – to treat the sides of the canvas as your first four lines. By touching them all before I start, I can orientate myself and feel my way into a composition.

[SL] You often use a window in your paintings; many artists have done this. You show us an intimate domestic interior – and then a landscape beyond.

[AM] There are echoes between inside and outside, a moving to and fro. The Danish and the Dutch understand the simple pleasure to be found in jugs, tables and chairs. Moving through the day as we all do – it is a wonderful thing to give it time, to watch it.

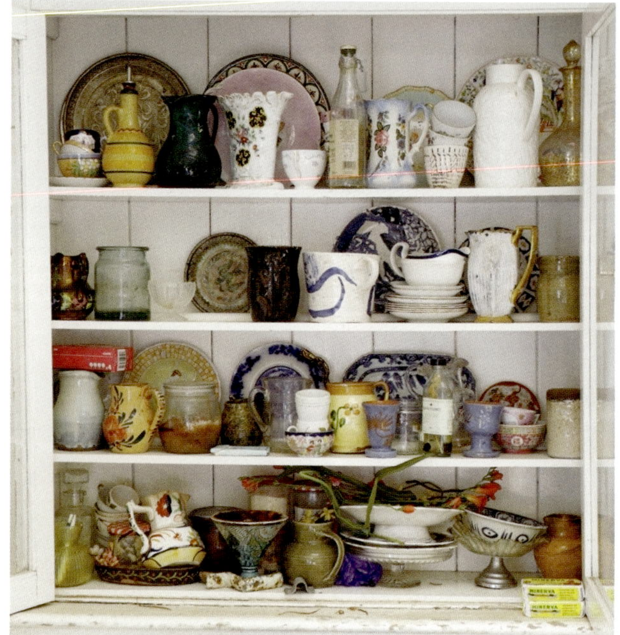

Alice's family dresser

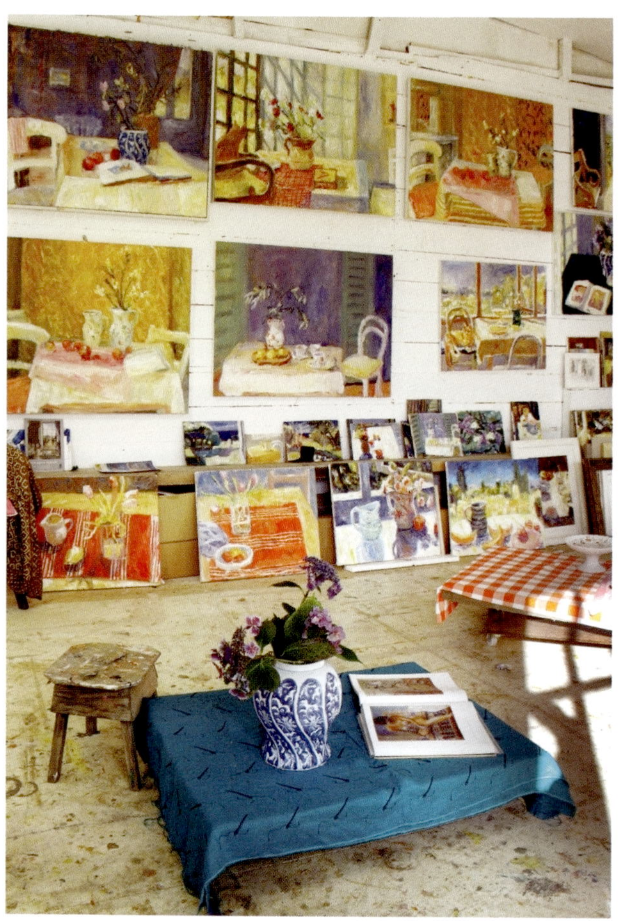

The studio at Polgrean Farm

Do you go back to the same forms? I am thinking of shapes in poetry.

[SL] I mostly write short poems in free verse with minimal punctuation. I tend towards reticence. But I need to keep on exploring different ideas. Maybe there can still be this spareness in longer poems. You can't stay still.

I am thinking about the places where we work. It strikes me that you need to work in a studio.

[AM] Yes, I am an observational painter. I need the physical space, being there.

[SL] I spent some time in your studio – with its dresser and tables, pots and jugs. It made me think how the objects we use every day, and might not even notice, are beautiful. You remind us of that.

Perhaps you don't have quite the freedom of the writer? I love being able to work anywhere. It is very liberating, although I do tend to work in a particular place – a room of my own – with wonderful morning light. It is another kind of ritual, to sit here at my desk. Listening, waiting.

RHYMES AND ECHOES

[SL] I am thinking back now. I would say that in these poems I was responding in language to your life and work as an artist and also to the place where you live and paint. Writing the poems enabled me to begin to see the world, briefly, through the eyes of a painter.

How did it work for you, Alice? I know you had anxieties about combining text and paintings.

[AM] The reticence of the poems was helpful and also the fact that neither was illustrative of the other. Painting and poem are just there with their space around them, without comment.

[SL] I am hoping that people will read a poem and look at a painting in a new way. They will be challenged a little.

There are echoes in our thinking, in our practice. For example, we discovered we were both interested in the idea of time in the making of work.

[AM] Rhymes and echoes also make me think of rhythm – the rhythm of making a painting. When I started painting as a job, I thought I ought to paint all the time. That may have been true then but now I realise that the intervals between painting are equally important. If I just paint I am not letting the puzzle work itself out – that needs time.

Then there are the larger patterns you see when you begin to assemble a body of work for an exhibition, say. This can help me see things I didn't see before.

[SL] And I am wondering how you chose the work for this exhibition.

[AM] I find something, see things I couldn't see before. I am interested in that revealing, that recognition.

[SL] It sounds similar to the process of putting together a collection of poetry. I find subtle connections – threads. So much is intuitive as you work and it is only later that you see the connections.

Some big questions. Why do you paint? Why do you think it matters?

[AM] Yes, you spend a lot of time on your own and sometimes you wonder, what is the point? I think for me it is an act of defiance, against my own doom and gloom. It is an act of joy. It is a shout out for beauty.

You do it because you need to. If I like a painting, it is striking that chord, it is speaking back to me. Sometimes I look at things in a museum and certain objects, even very simple things, have that effect on me. The intent of the maker comes through.

[SL] This reminds me of Rainer Maria Rilke, and what he writes in his *Letters to a Young Poet*. He tells Kappus (the young poet) that he must feel the necessity to write; it must be a way of being. Rilke tells him of the loneliness of the creative life, that the artist must look within and not pay too much heed to the opinions of others. He advises him 'not to seek the answers but to live the questions'.

Perhaps if we paint or write like this we may just occasionally make something that will enable others to see the world through someone else's eyes, to understand a little more about our humanity. And that must be a good thing.

paintings & poems

Telling colour

I pick up shells

tellins, scallops
limpets, saddle oysters –

look for words for colour

apricot, rose, ochre, tangerine
chalk, sand –

find them again
in a sunset, away across

Tresco and Bryher

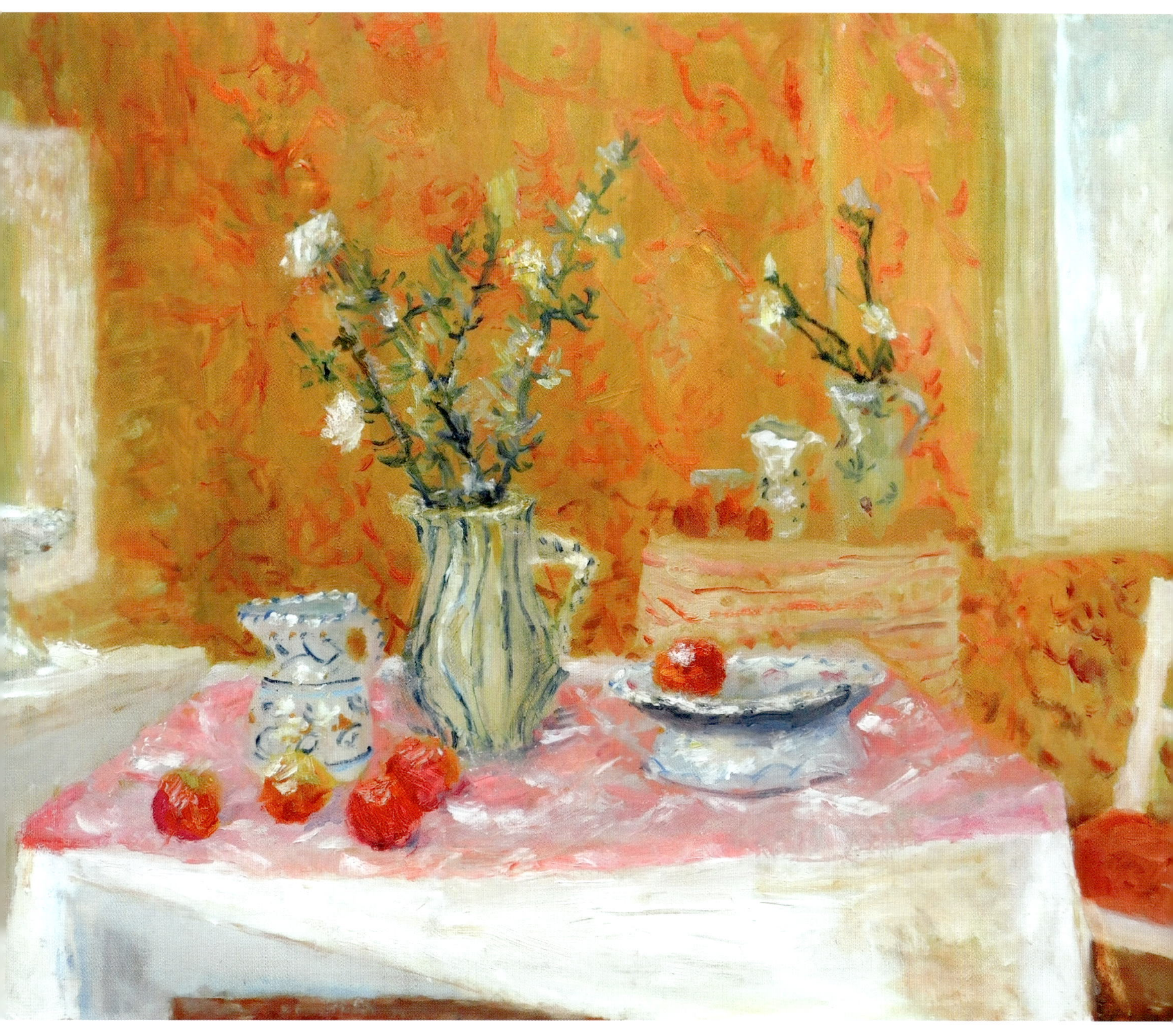

Earth Yellows and Pink · 2022 · oil on canvas · 80 x 100 cm

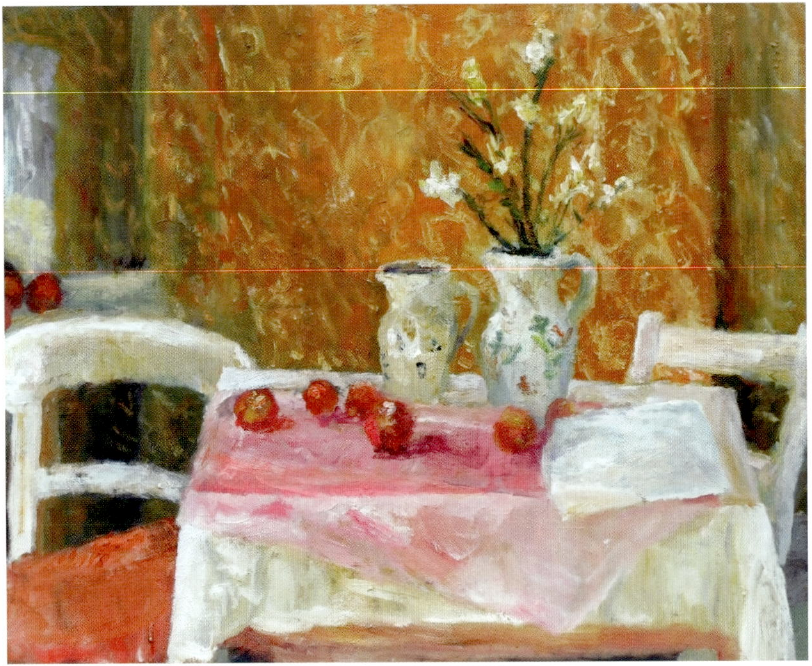

Warm Yellows in the Studio · 2022–3 · oil on canvas · 80 x 100 cm

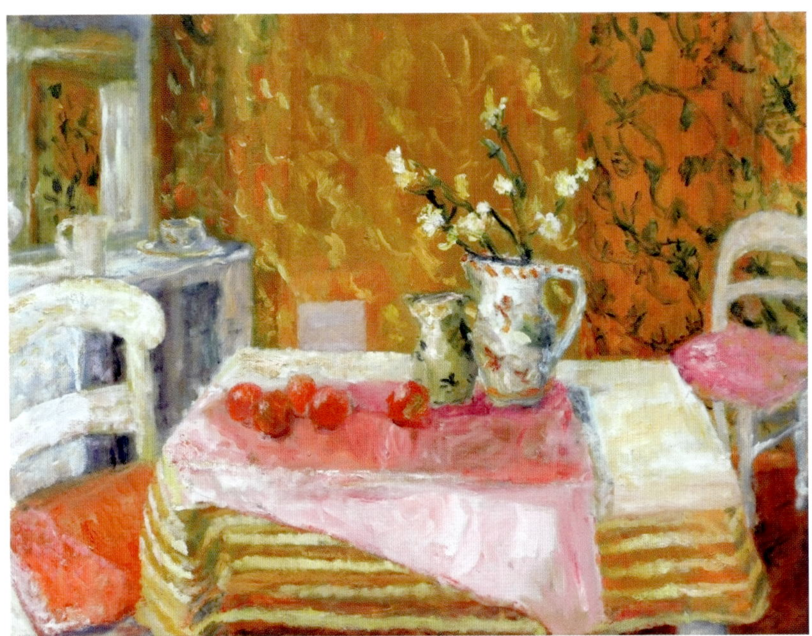

Double Pink · 2022–3 · oil on canvas · 75.5 x 105 cm

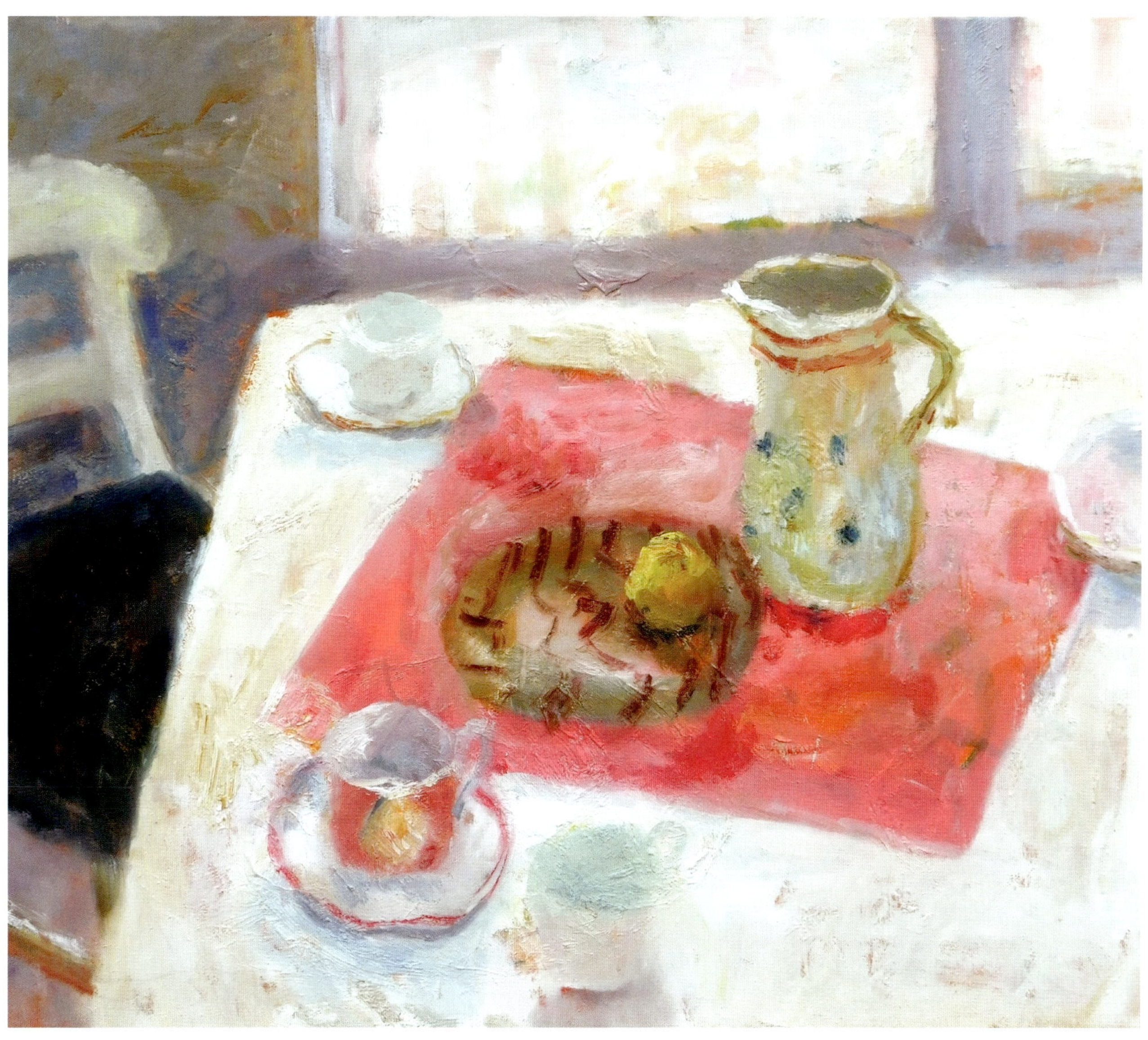

The Zig-Zag Plate and Pink Cloth · 2022–3 · oil on canvas · 60 x 70 cm

14th May

two swarms today
(noisy black clouds, bees busy
about their business)

one pours, a slow brown river
under the slates of the house

Alice, I wish you could collect
the other that is now
quiet in the old cherry tree

the bees could live in your orchard
in the skep you were making
from straw and bramble

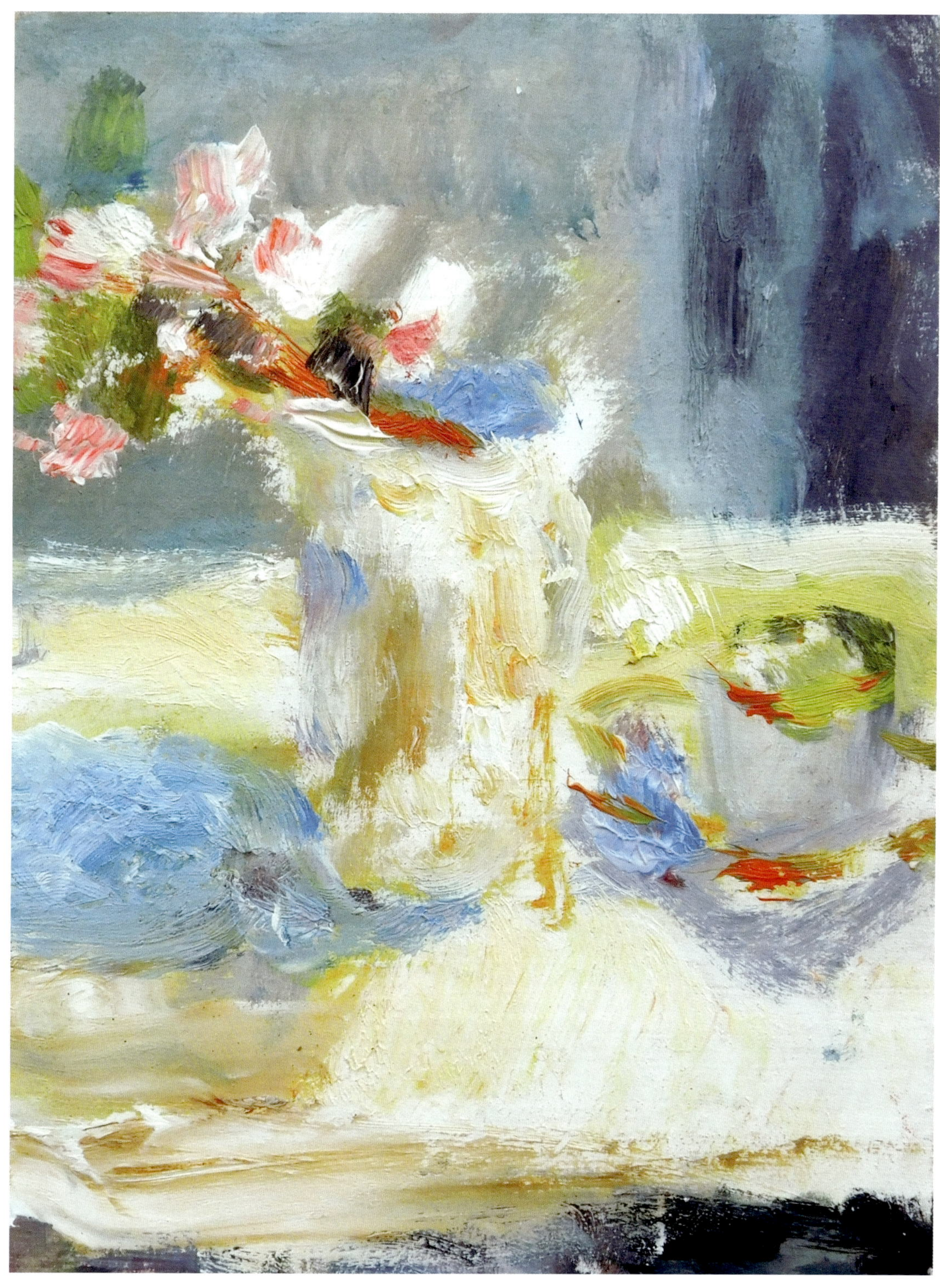

Apple Blossom · 2022 · oil on board · 20 x 15 cm

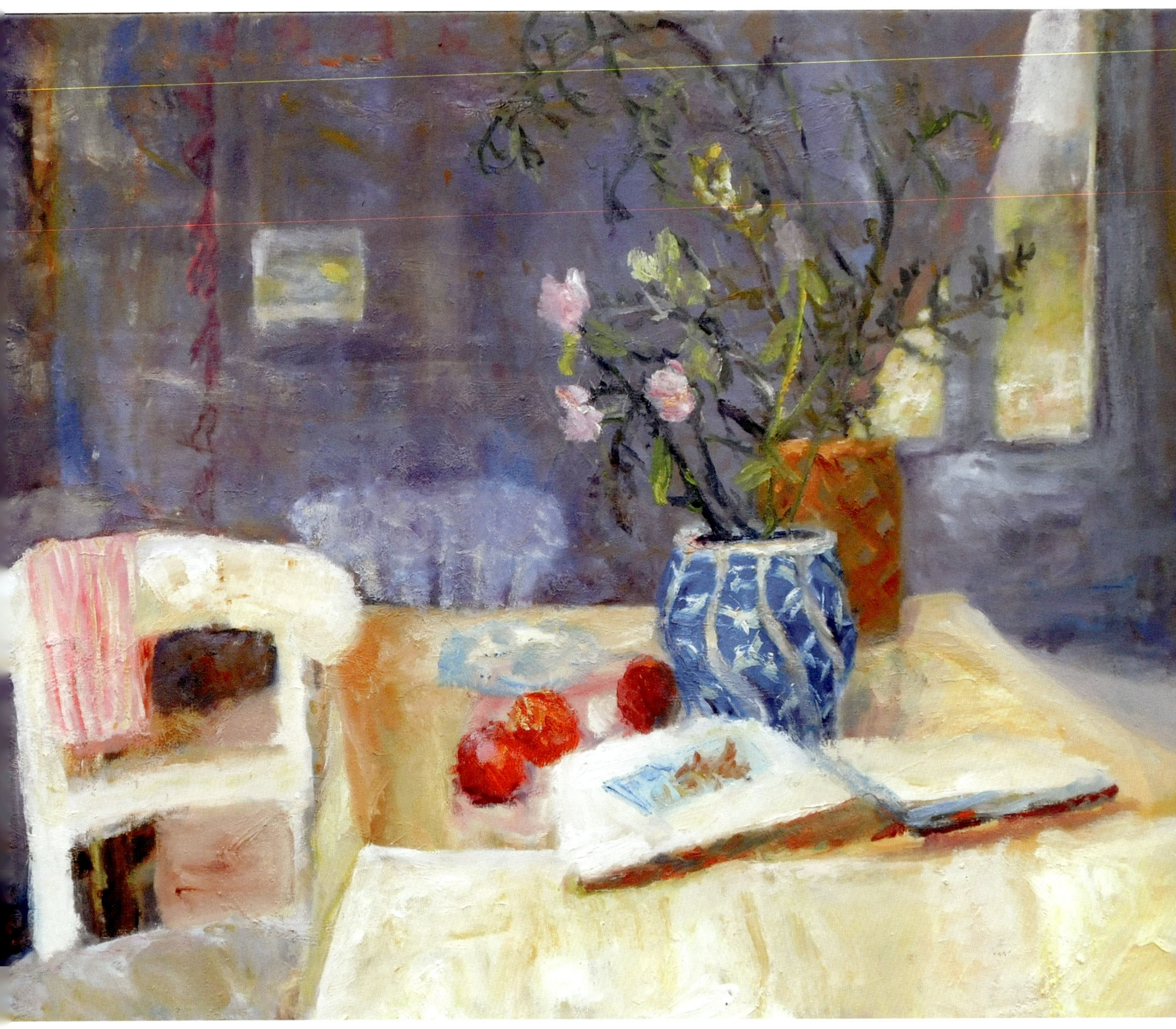

The New Blue and White Vase · 2022–3 · oil on canvas · 80 x 100.5 cm

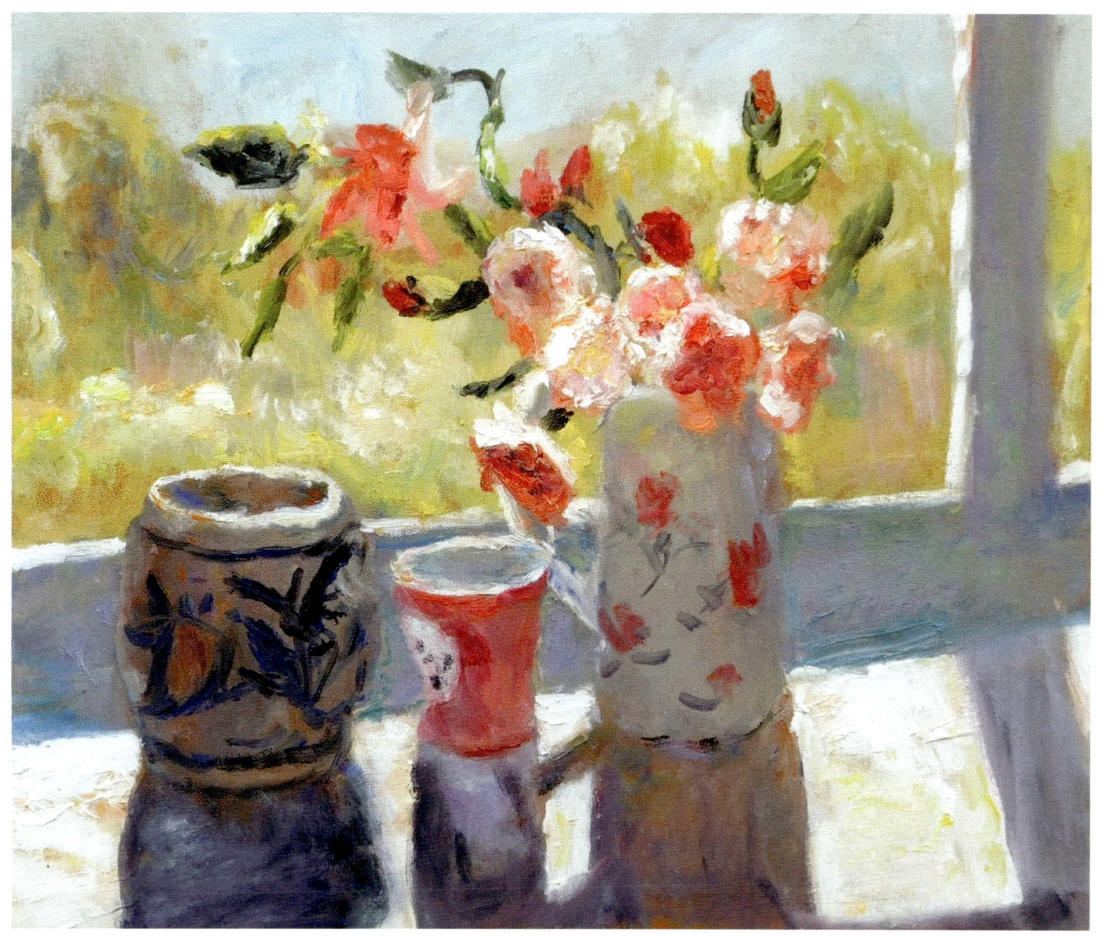

First Roses · 2022 · oil on canvas · 50 x 60 cm

early roses

blush noisette, I think –

all those dense cupped petals
that small cluster of yellow stamens
at its heart

you have put the roses
in a lustre jug that glints
in this morning's sunlight,

does a painting have a scent –
if so, this one is
musk, clove

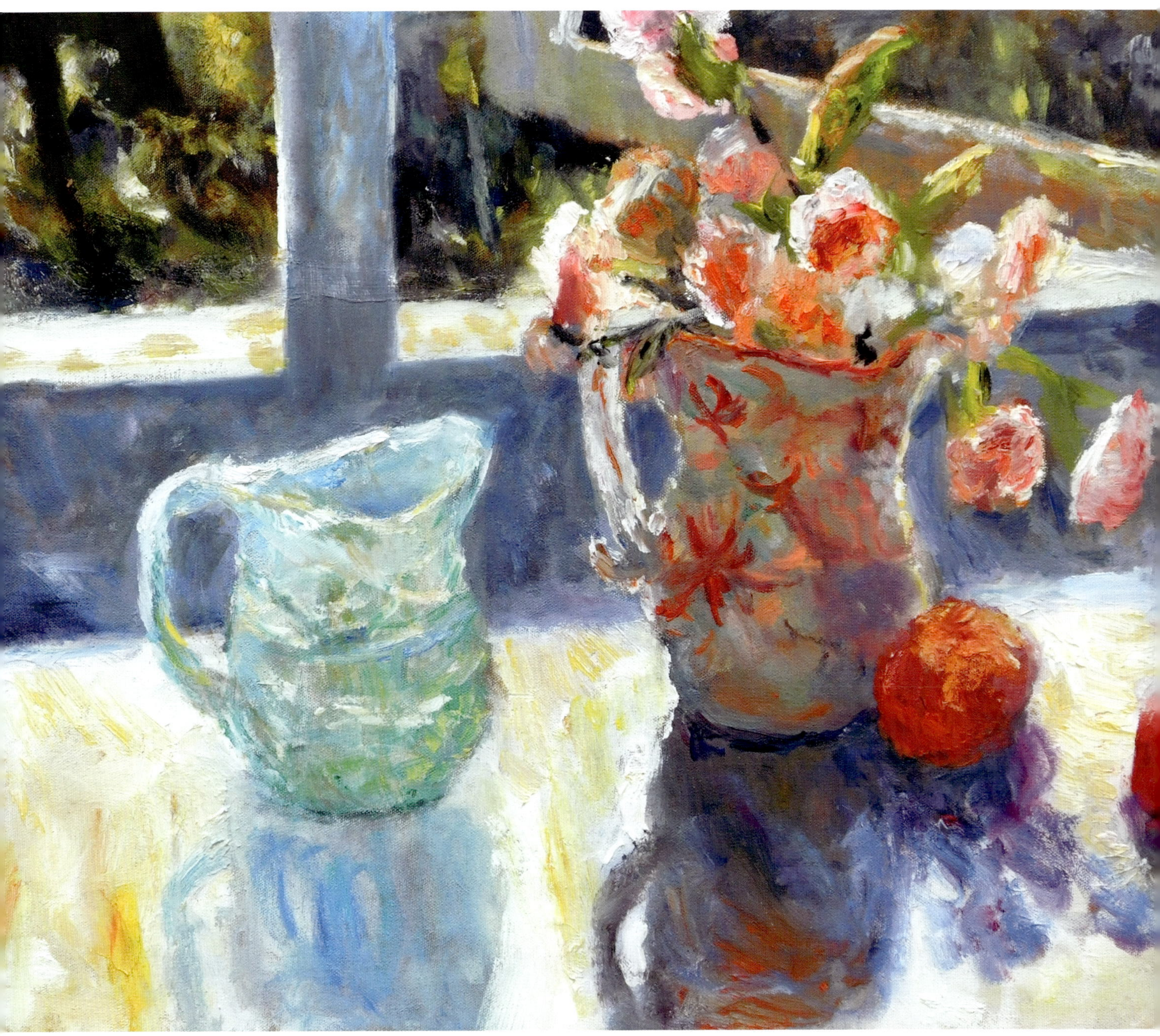

Bright Sunlight on Early Roses · 2022 · oil on canvas · 50 x 60 cm

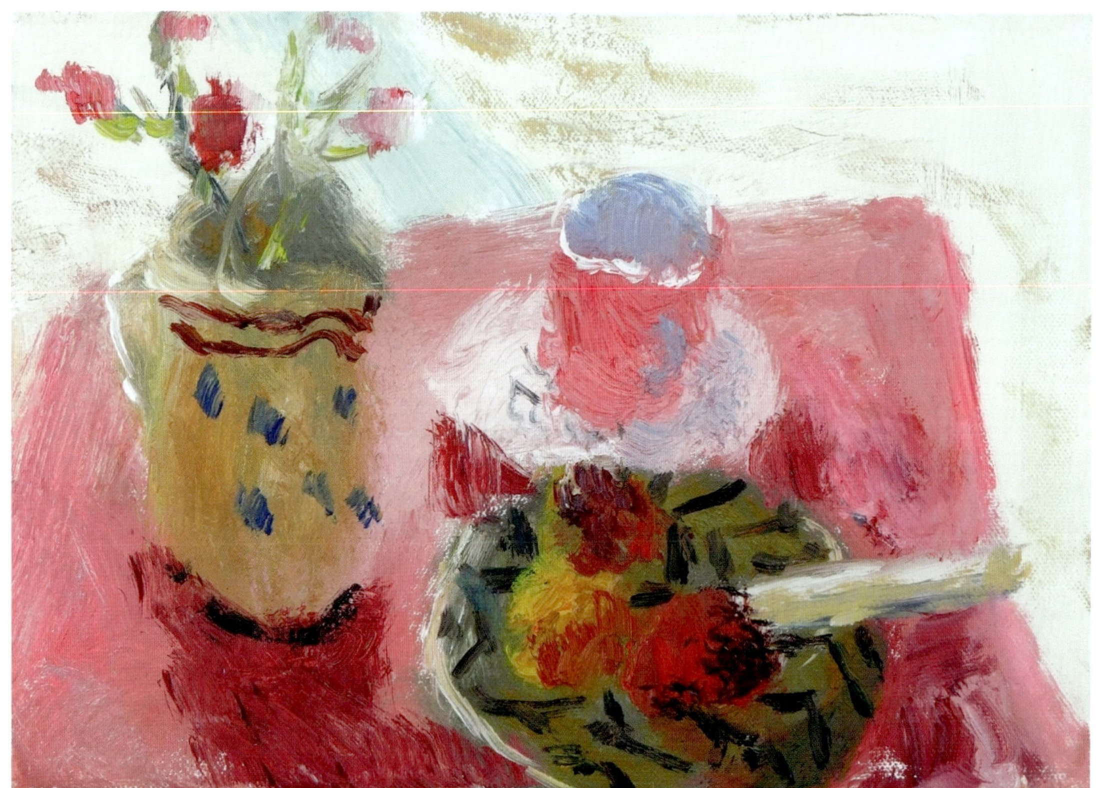

Pink and Reds · 2023 · oil on canvas · 21 x 30 cm

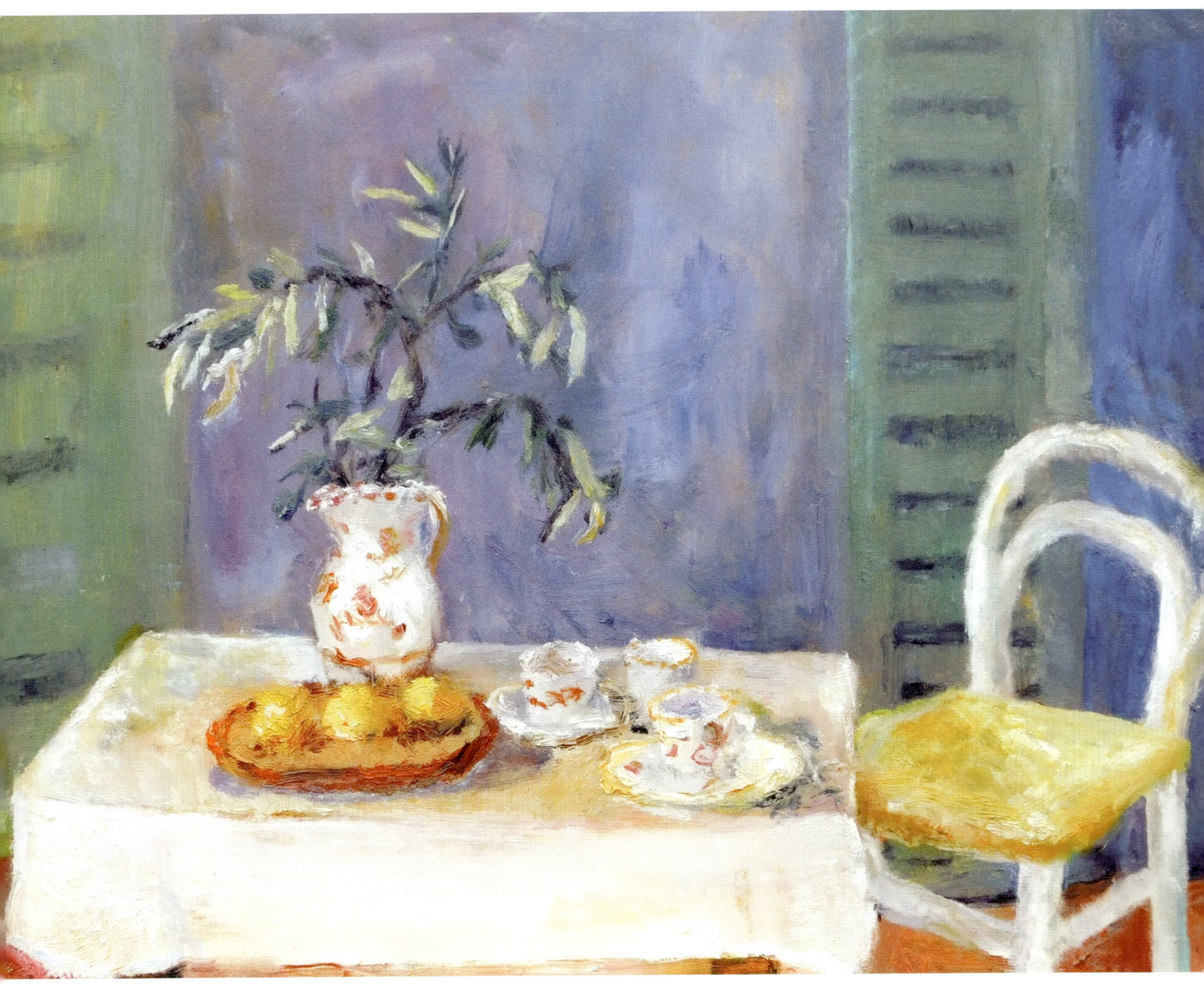

The Jade Green Shutters, Lemons and Olive Branch · 2022 · oil on canvas · 76 x 100 cm

room

stanza, in Italian –

we both inhabit them
dwell among their shapes, spaces

sometimes we open their windows
let in the scent of rain

or free a frantic bee
into the wide blue air –

sometimes we dance in them

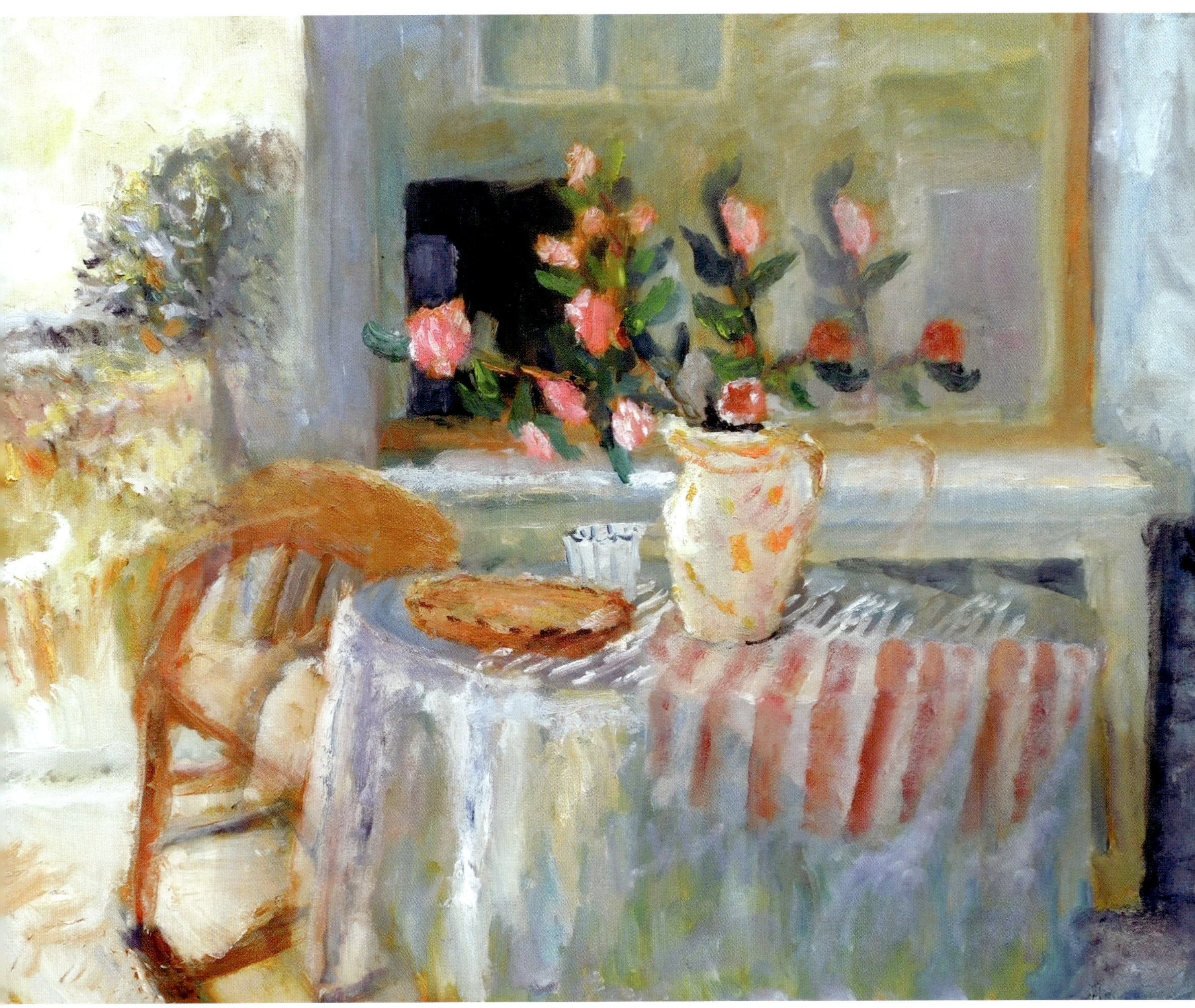

Spring Warmth and Camellias · 2023 · oil on canvas · 76 x 100 cm

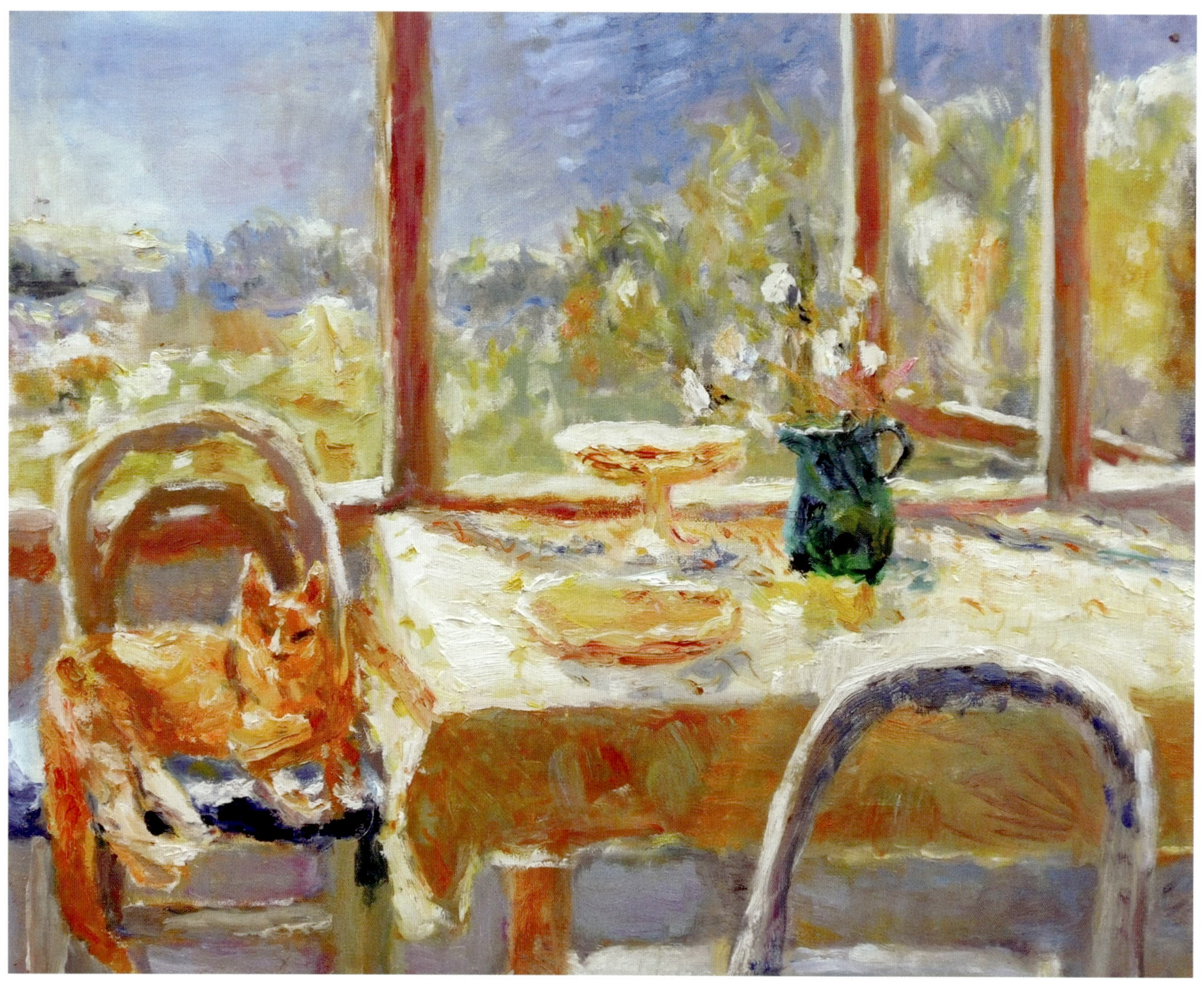

Sleeping in Summer Warmth · 2022 · oil on canvas · 61 x 76 cm

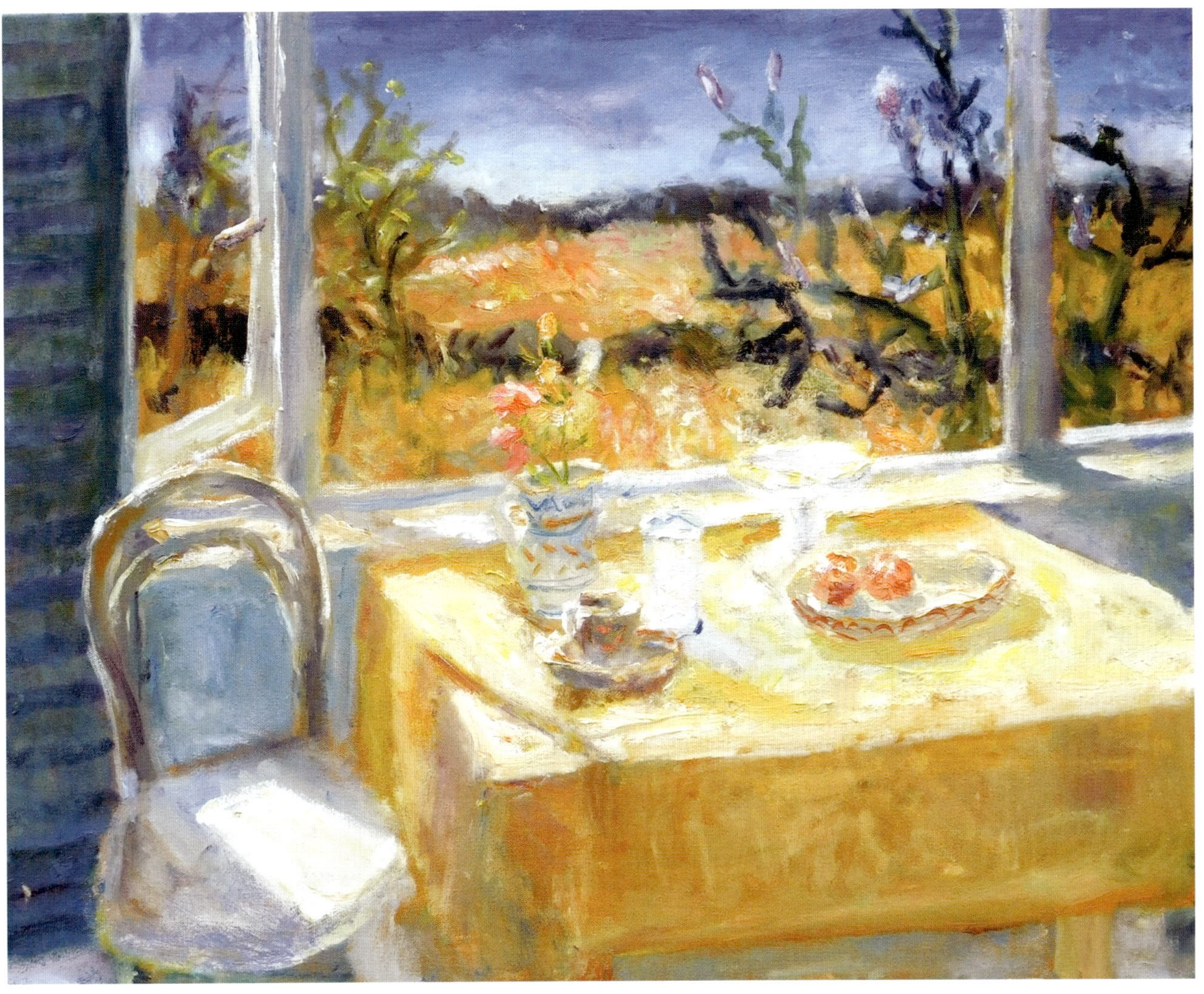

Cool Studio and Geranium · 2022 · oil on canvas · 60 x 76 cm

Chysauster, over the Red River

where our Iron Age ancestors
built their courtyard houses
worked the small fields
kept goats perhaps,
tending and making, the rhythms
of our lives

archaeologists found pottery bowls
there, a glass bead, stone tools,
and some water-worn pebbles
of cream-coloured quartz
that you or I might have picked up
and taken home

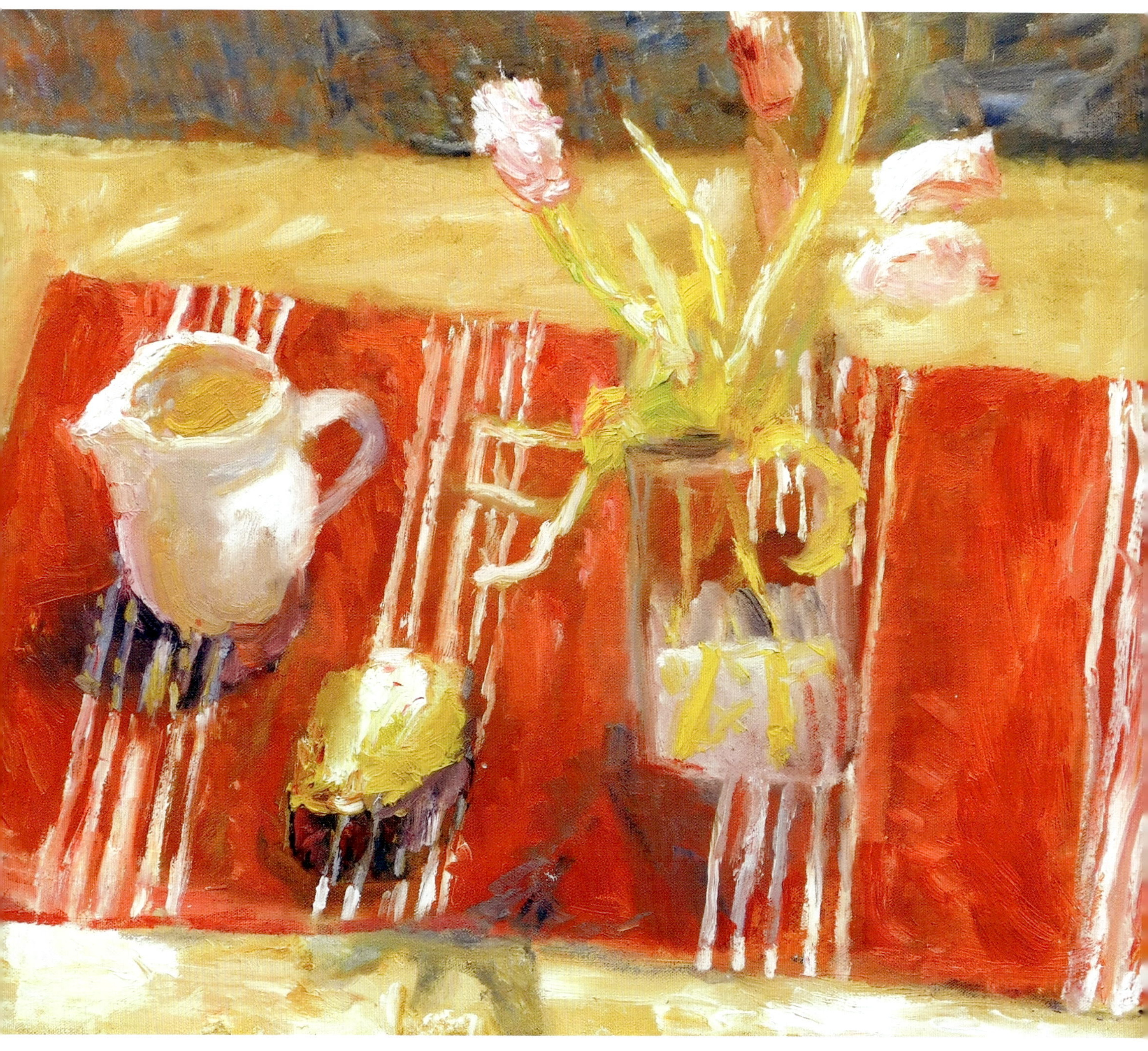

The Red and White Striped Cloth · 2022 · oil on canvas · 50 x 60 cm

overleaf · *High Summer Heat with Pieces of Melon* [detail] · 2022–3 · oil on canvas · 75 x 90 cm

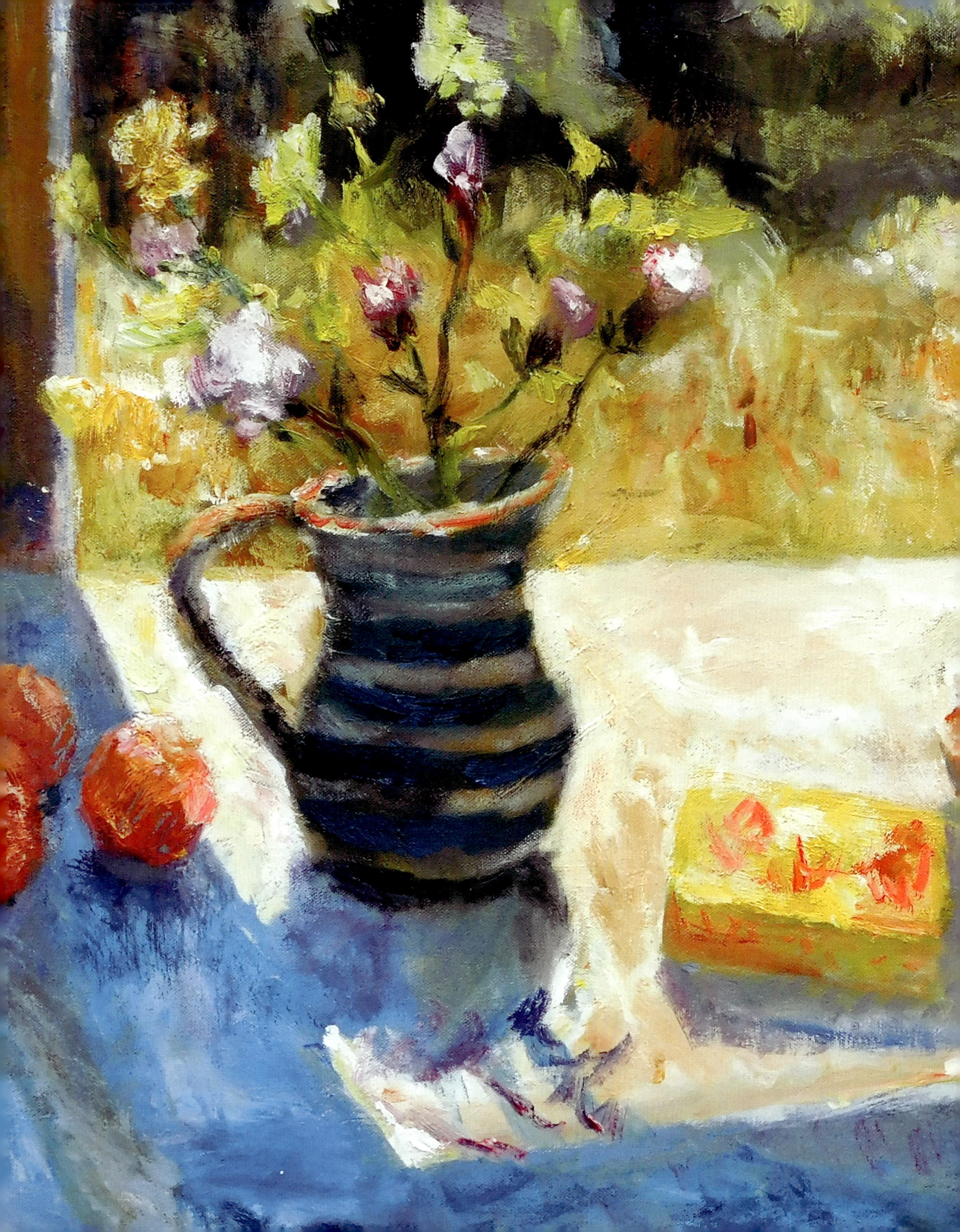

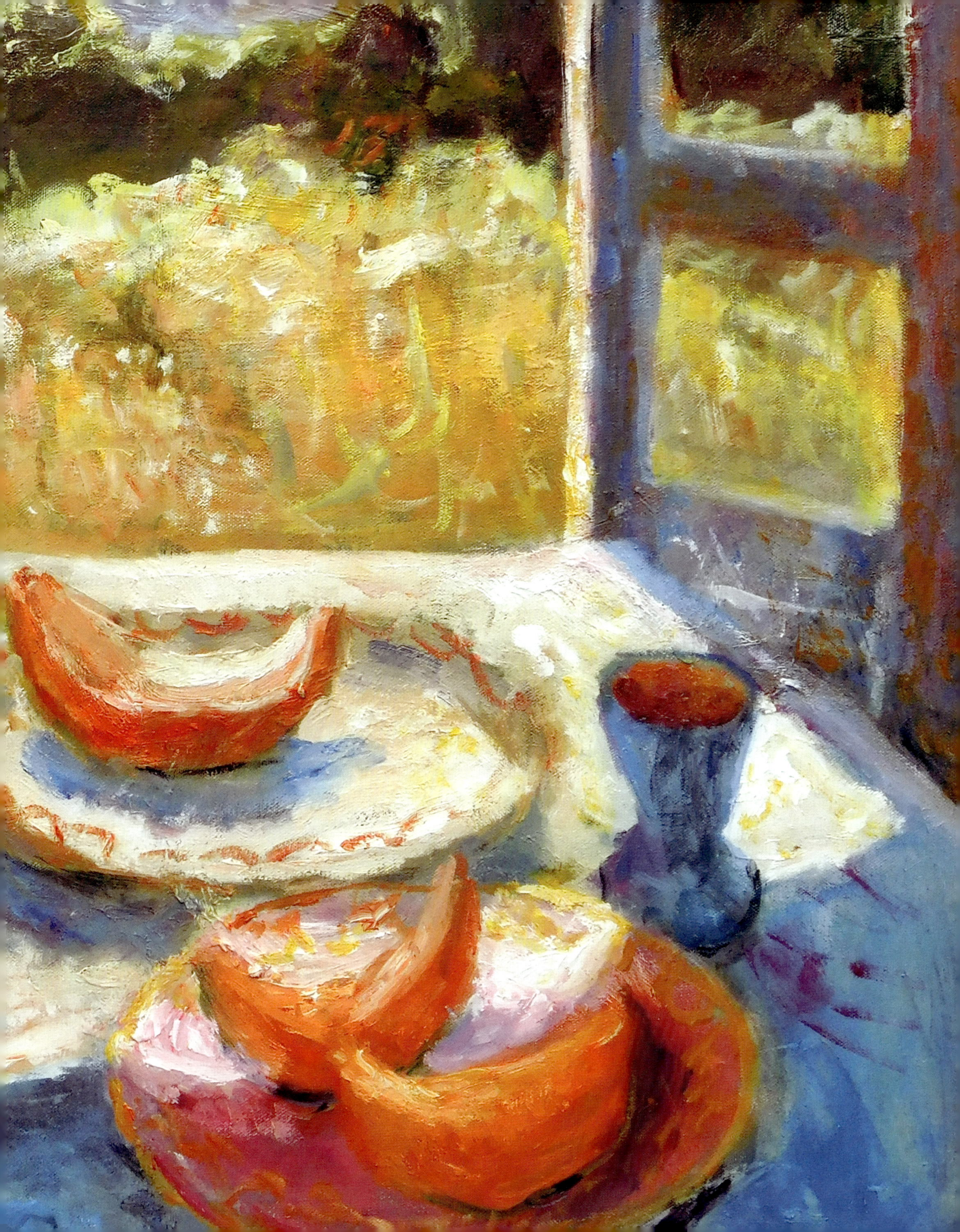

Here

I had been thinking about paradise
on this earth
how it might be a house by the sea,
(the quiet order within I sensed once
in a Benedictine monastery),
sun-filled rooms, a door
open to the leaping world

but this morning I could believe
it was here
spring almost beginning
the first flower
of the nectarine (perfectly balanced
on its bare branch)
opening, opening

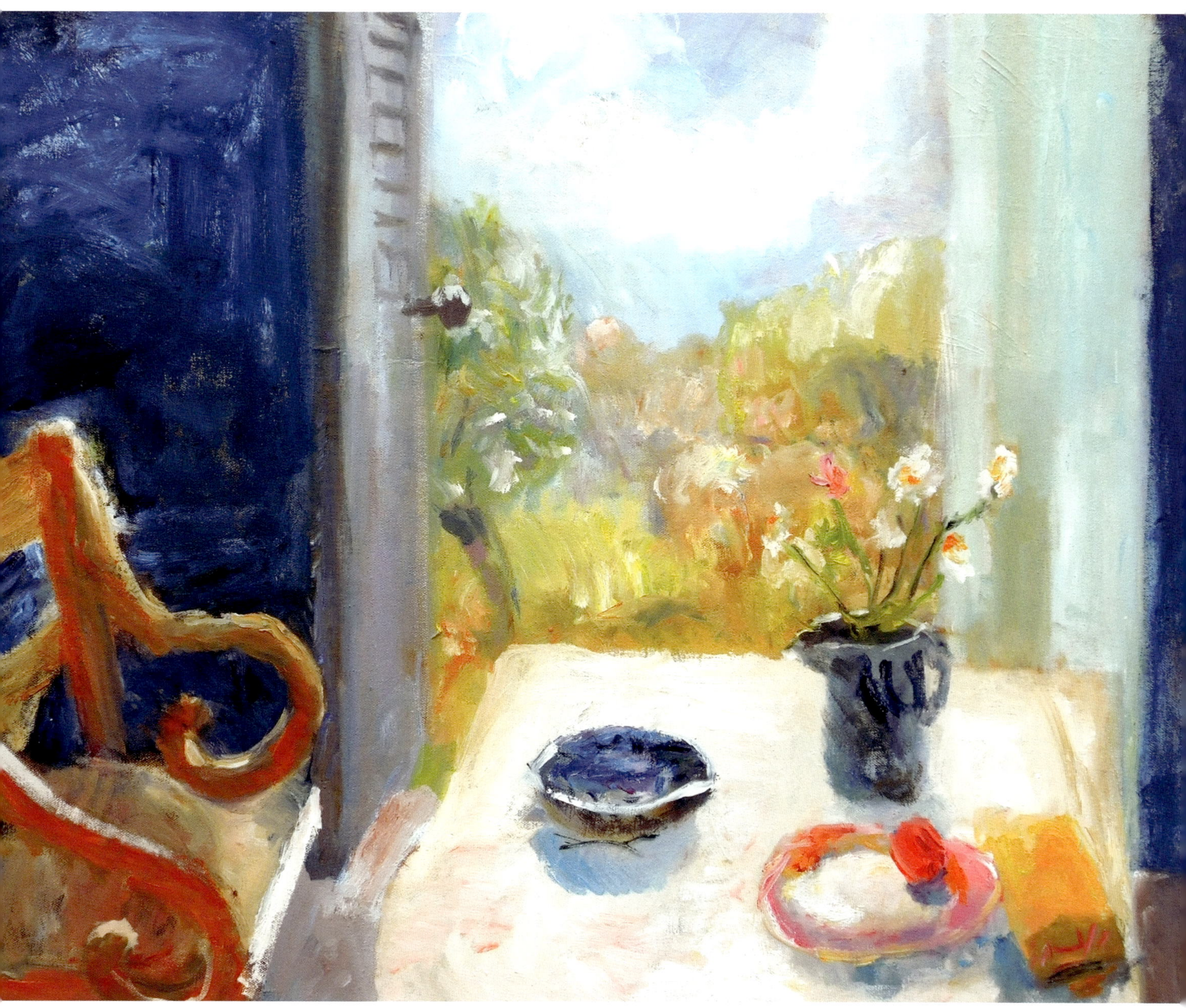

Indigo to Apricot · 2022 · oil on canvas · 60 x 76 cm

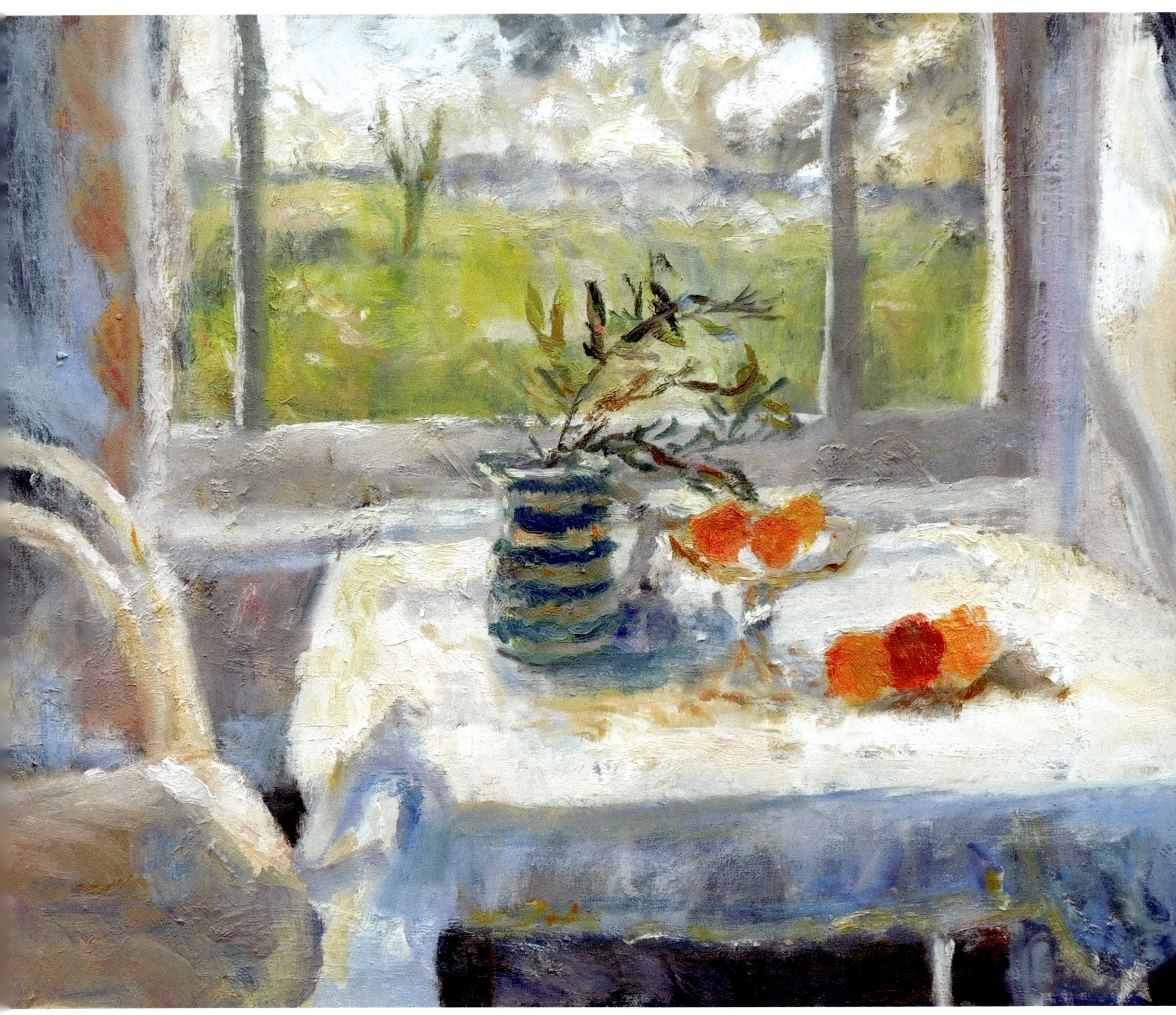

Olive Branch · 2021 · oil on canvas · 61 x 76 cm

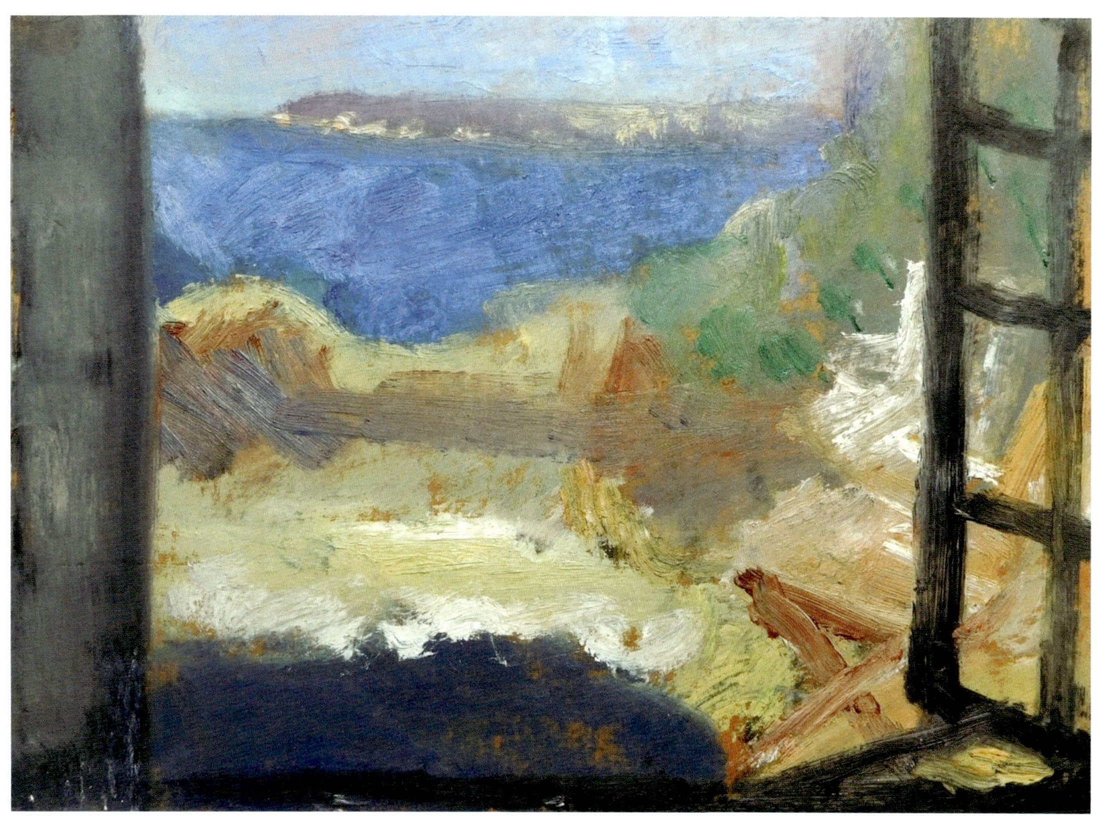

Open Window by the Sea · 2022 · oil on board · 22.5 x 30 cm

someone has put a sprig
of blossom in a jug
bought butter
small sweet oranges
soon there will be a
cake of almond
and orange peel
there will be a kettle
on the stove,
the rain will drench the garden

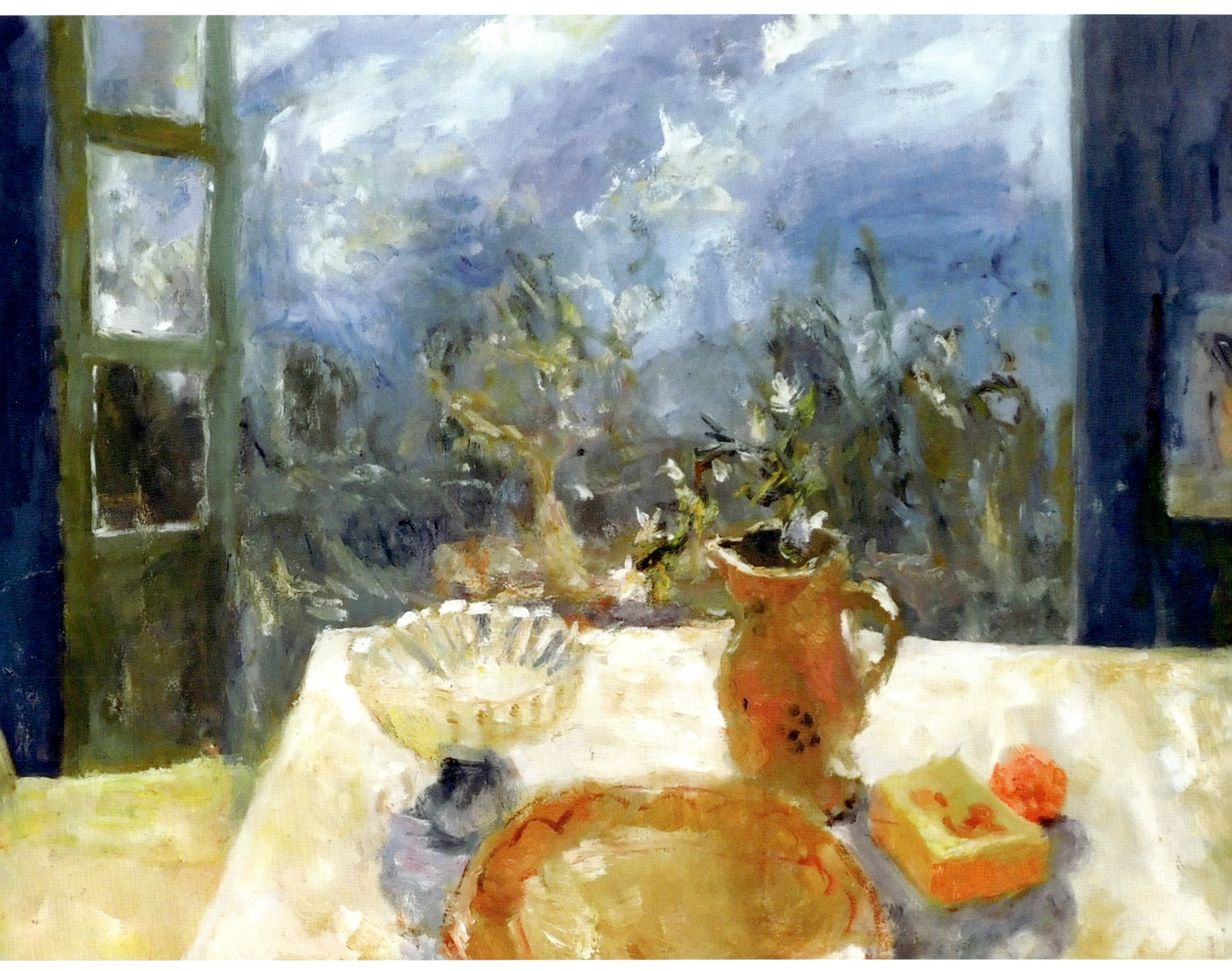

First Day of Opening the French Windows · 2022 · oil on canvas · 80 x 100 cm

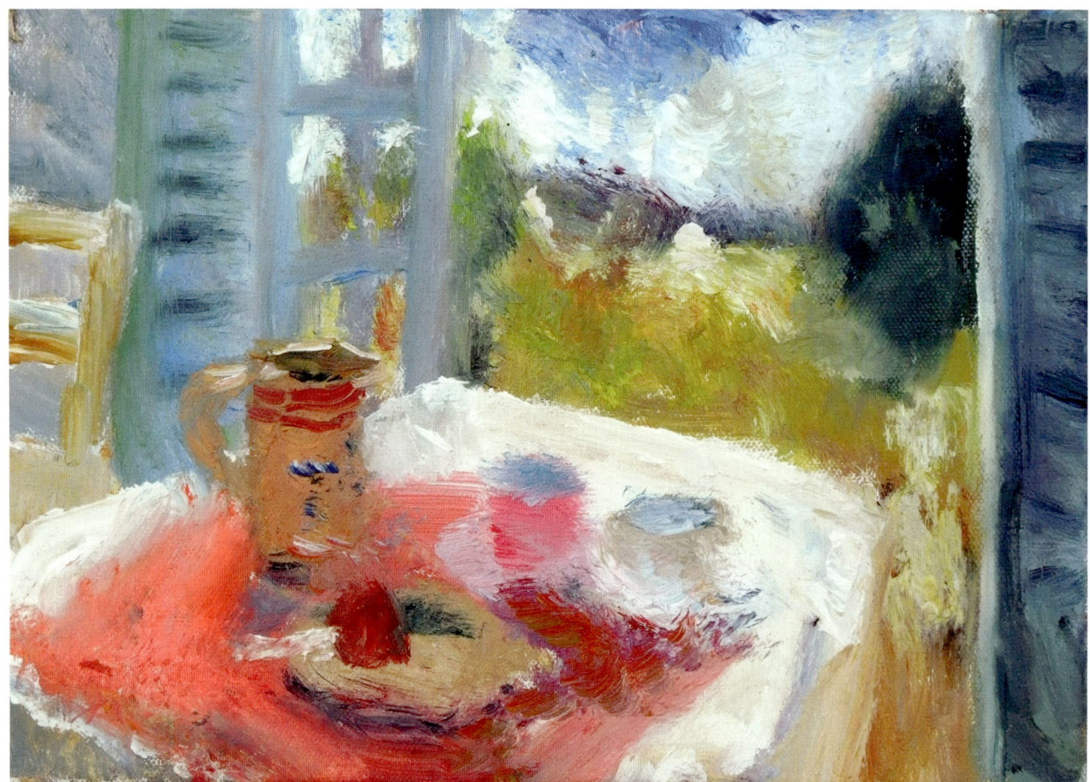

Fresh Air · 2022 · oil on canvas · 21 x 30 cm

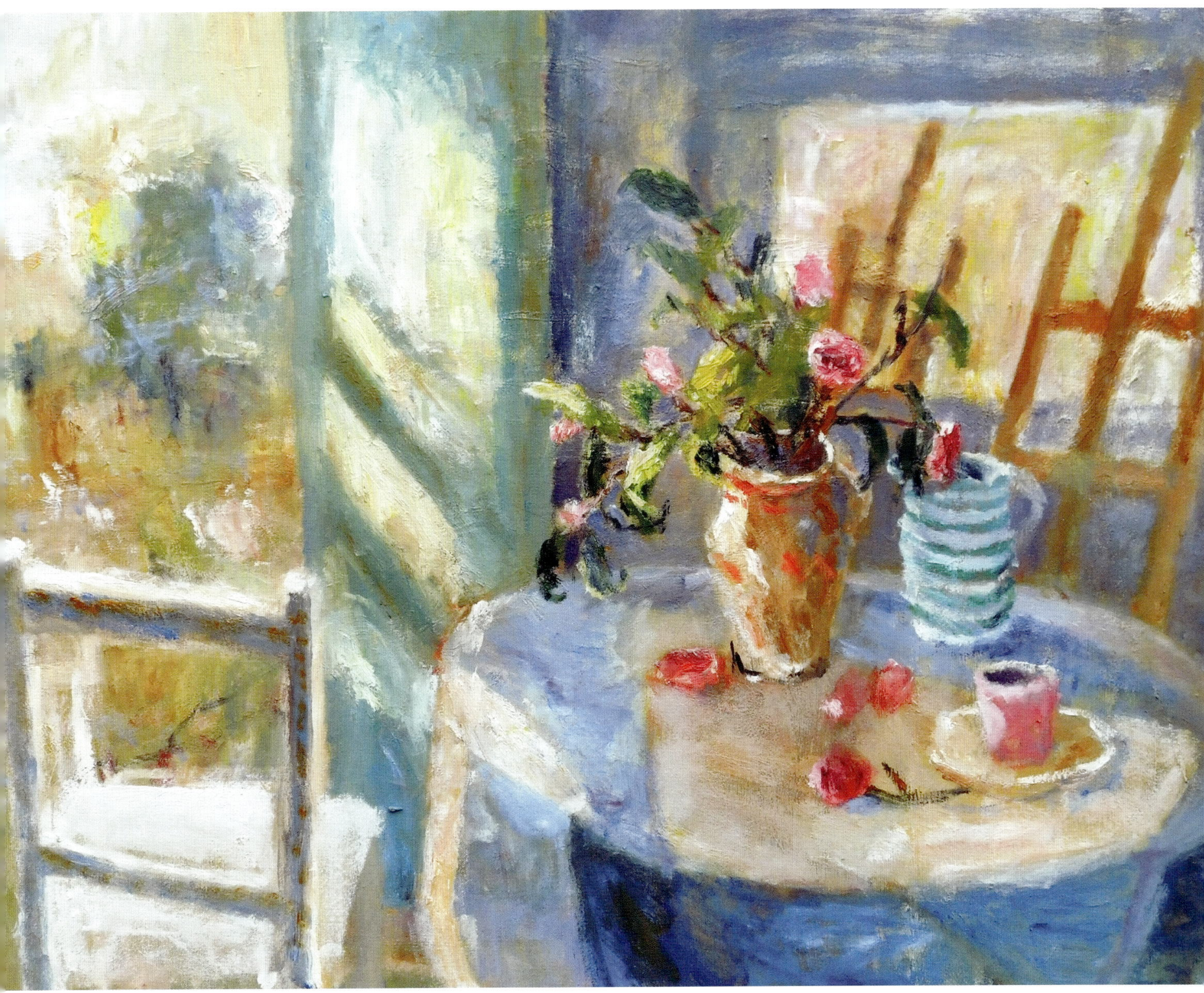

Solace · 2023 · oil on canvas · 76 x 100 cm

from what I remember, walking

Godrevy lighthouse (Mrs Ramsay knitting socks for the
lighthouse-keeper's children) – the sea, a blue cloth in want of
ironing – seals lolling on pale yellow sand – an adder in the dunes
– glow-worms at Gwithian, a match struck in the dark – St Ives, Ia's
town (her sailing here from Ireland on a leaf), artists' town – Wallis
painting for company on cardboard, tin, anything – Hepworth's
overalls still hanging in her studio, her garden seen through *Two
Forms (Divided Circle)* – a chapel on the headland for the saint of
seafarers, a light before lighthouses – sea thrift at West Penwith,
bracken in Bronze Age fields – meadow pipits' shrill trilling –
inland a trail of hamlets trip off the tongue: Trevail, Trevega,
Tremedda – a mermaid holds her mirror in St Senara's church
at Zennor – museum in miller's house, photographs of Lawrence
and Frieda at Tregerthen Farm in wartime, Katherine Mansfield
mourning her brother – I, mine

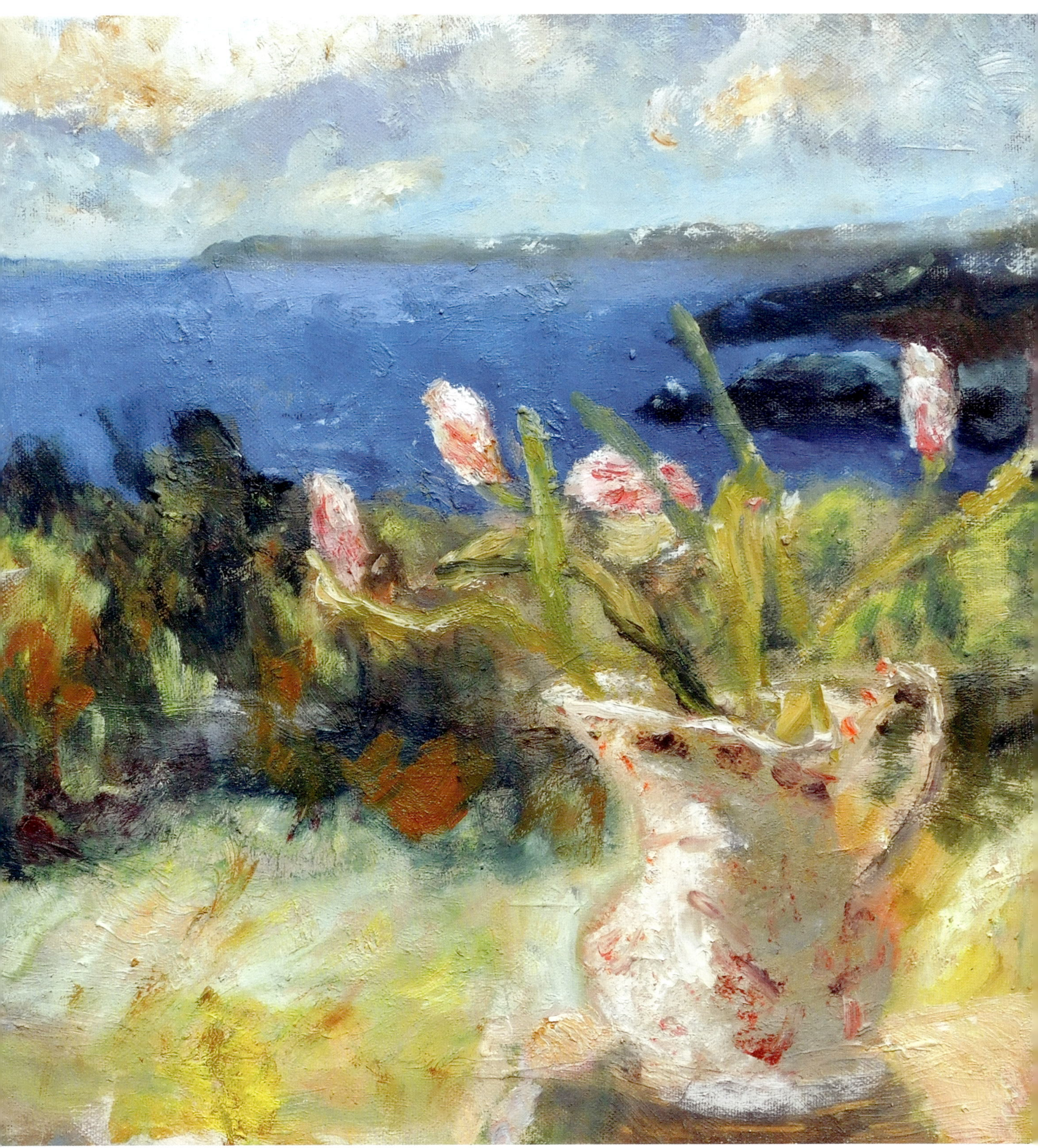

South West · 2022 · oil on canvas · 40 x 40 cm

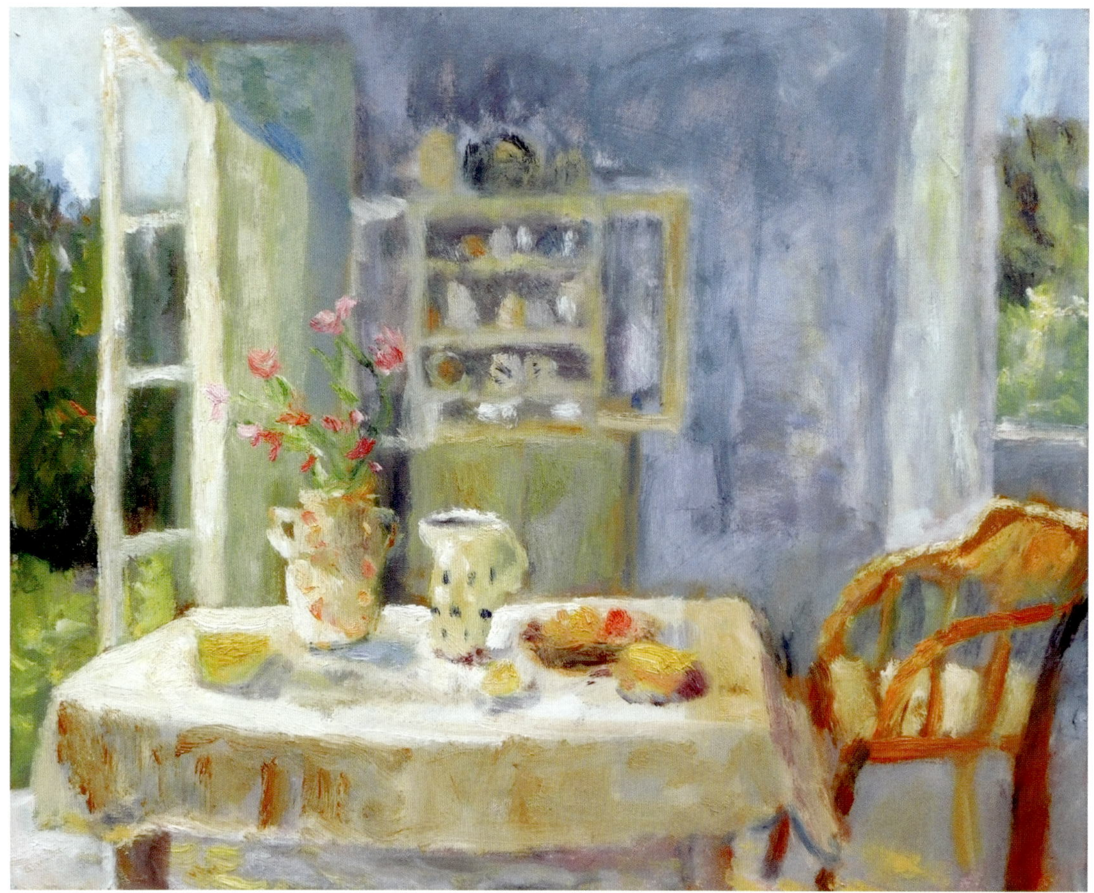

Sunny Studio · 2022 · oil on canvas · 61 x 76 cm

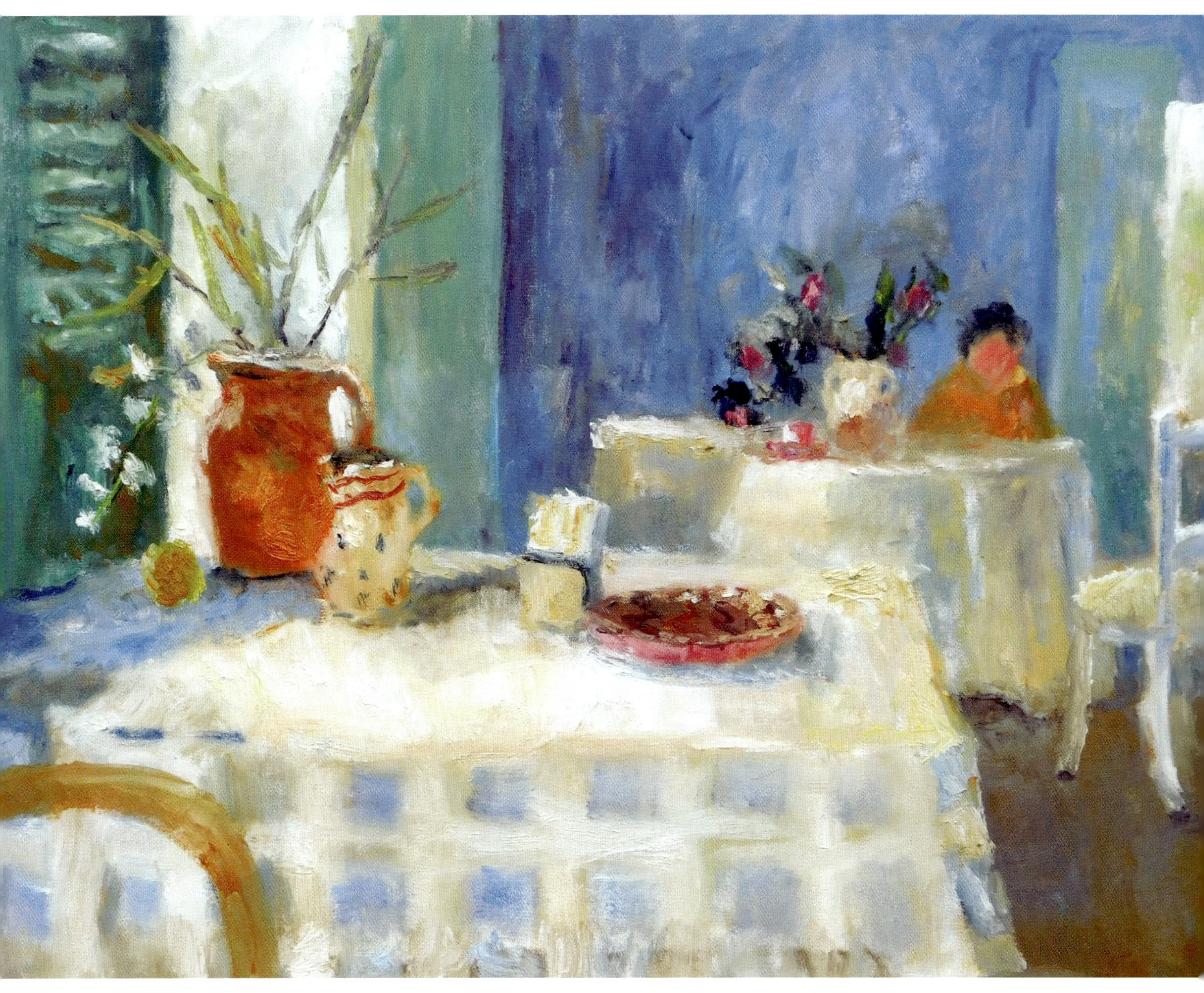

Reading Quietly · 2023 · oil on canvas · 76 x 100 cm

overleaf · *The Yellow and White Striped Cloth* [detail] · 2022 · oil on canvas · 76 x 100 cm

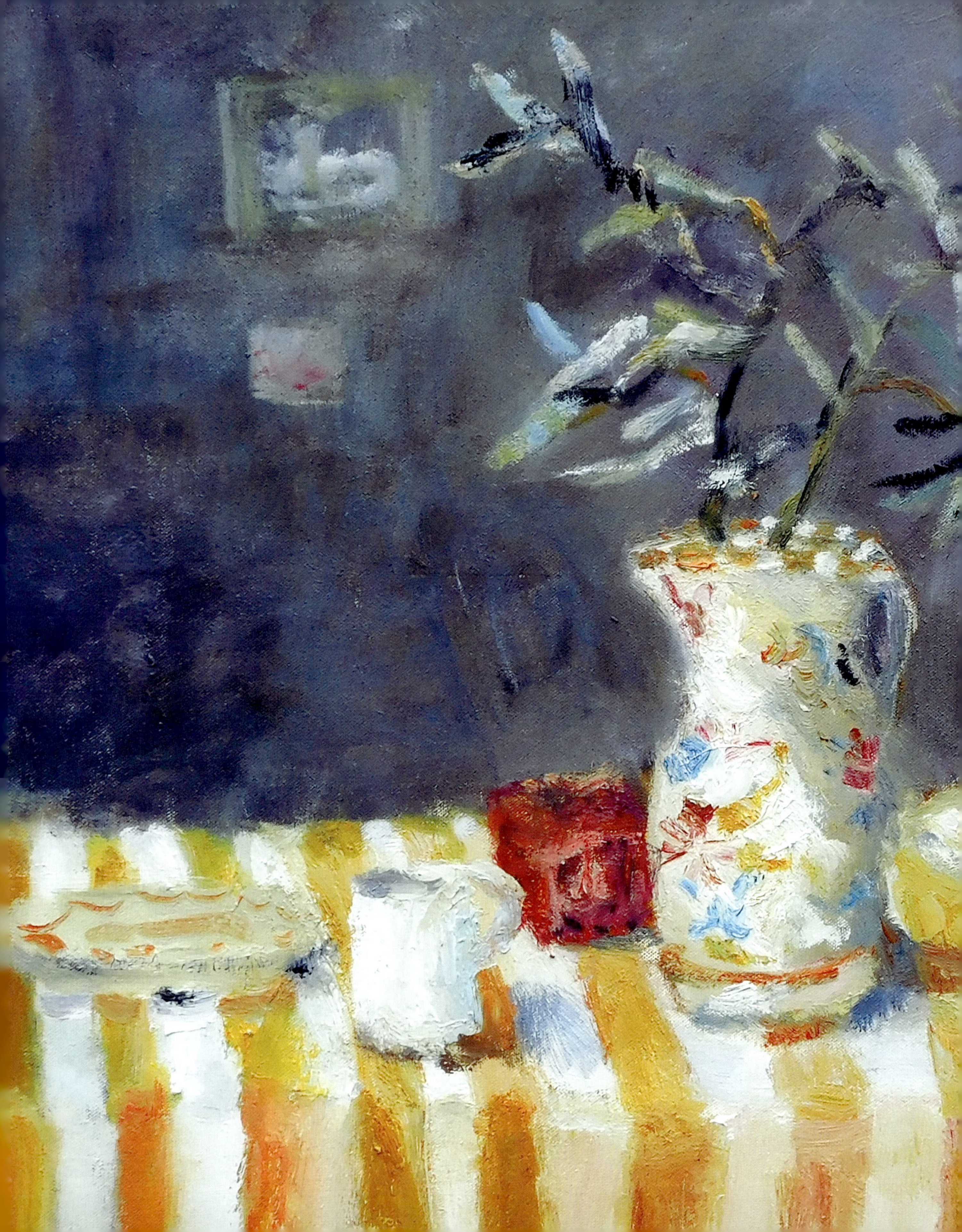

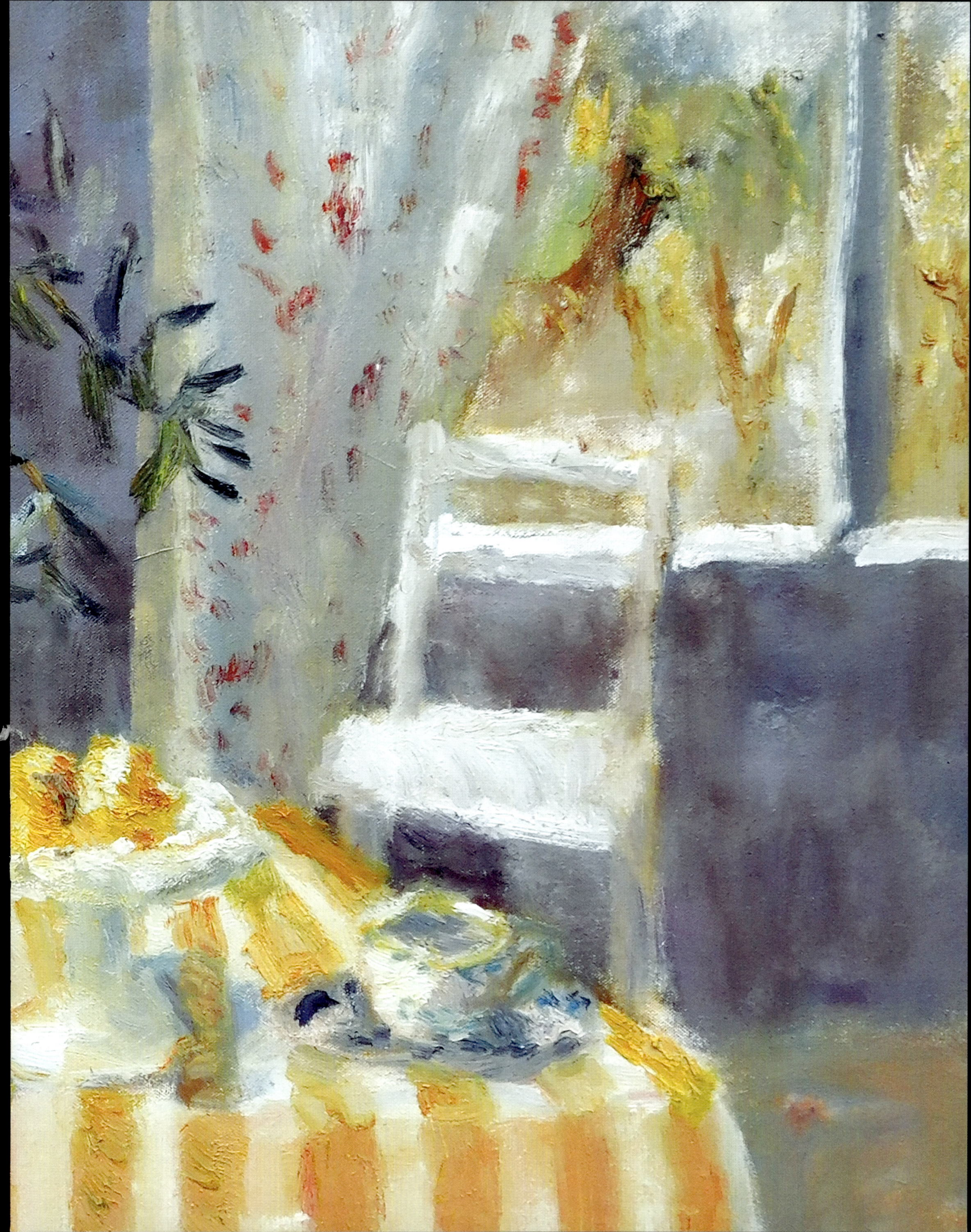

You have borrowed the sea
pinks and bluebells
for the cloth and pot
in your painting
that violet-
blue from the spring squill
and those whites
from the stitchwort
which Cornish children
call adder's spit,
old man's shirt

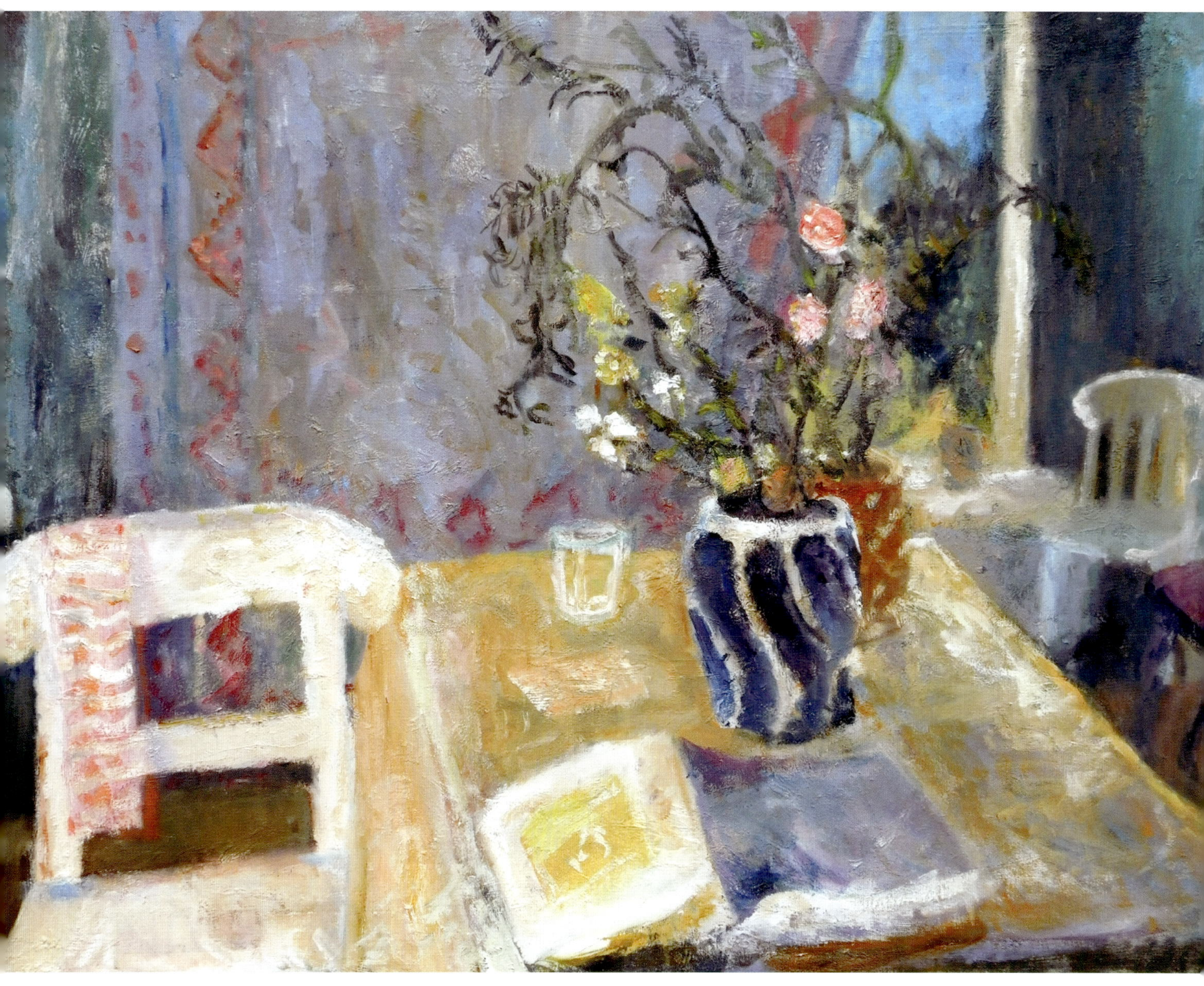

Looking at a Book · 2021–2 · oil on canvas · 76 x 101 cm

I sleep

with the curtains open
even in winter
I like to sense the frost whitening
the lawn,
the slow river, the creatures
deep in their leaves,
to know there is only glass
between me and the world outside
and besides, tonight I would have missed
the moon, how it lay
for a while its light,
on my hand, my pillow

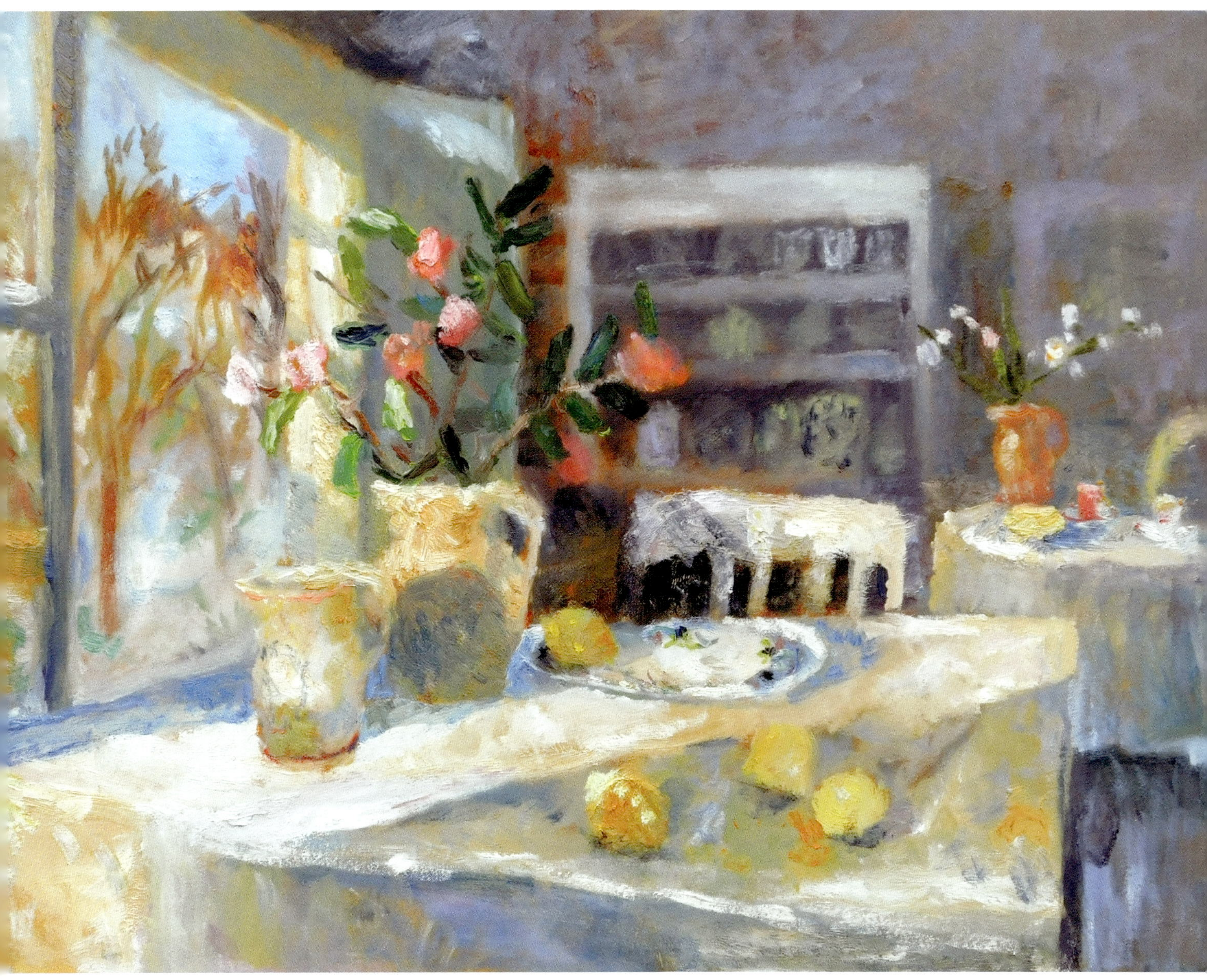

The Blues of Frost Outside · 2023 · oil on canvas · 76 x 100 cm

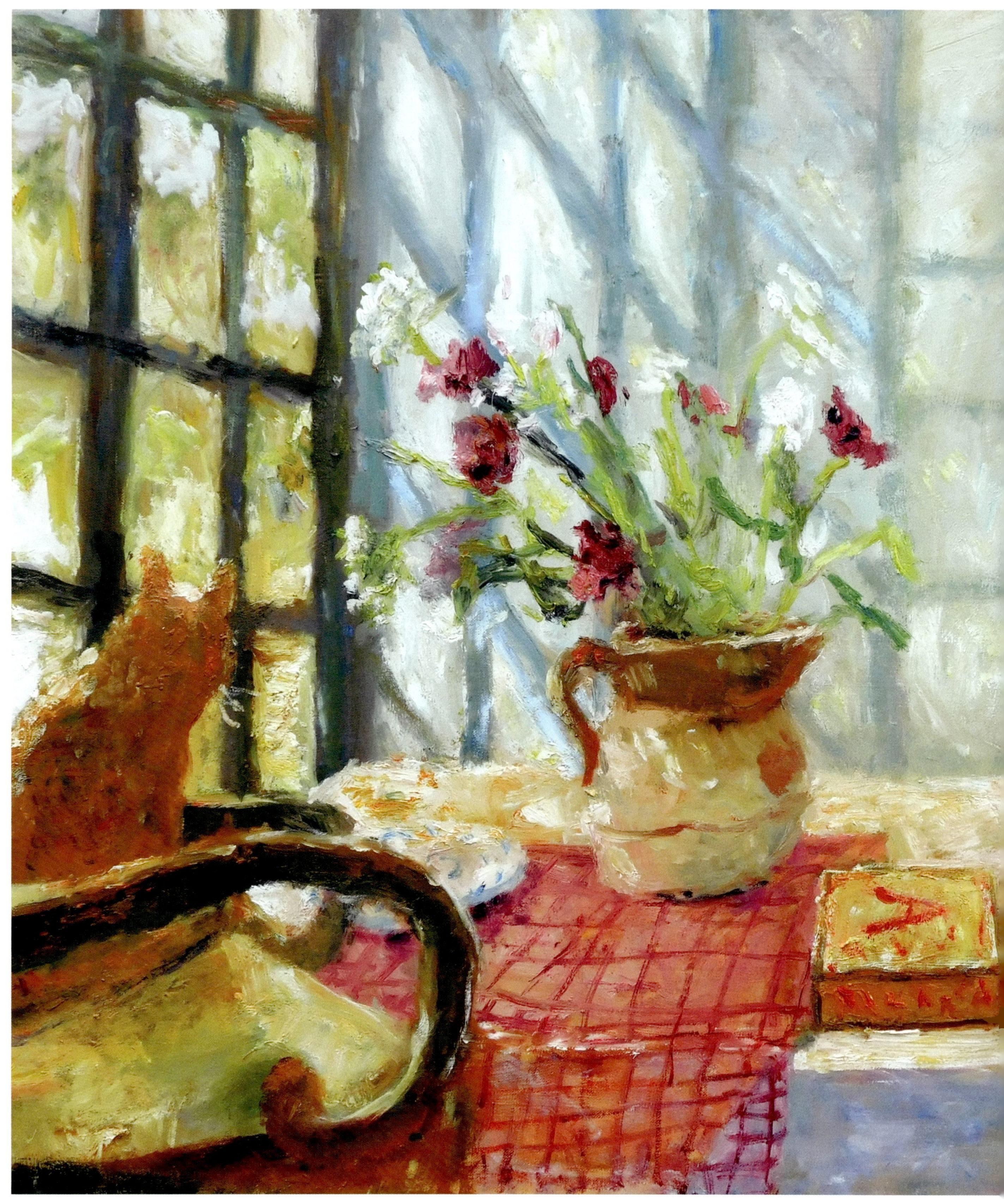

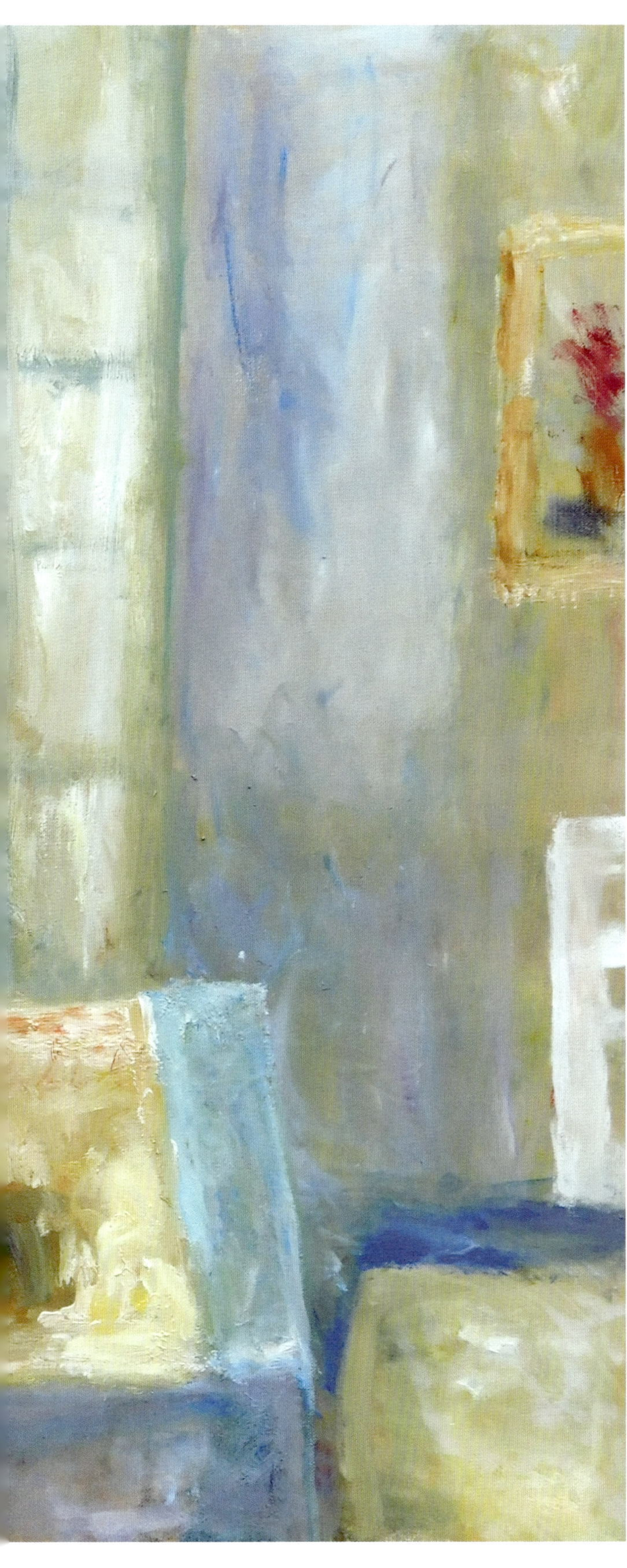

First Warmth · 2022 · oil on canvas · 76 x 100 cm

jasmine and blue haiku

white petals fallen
on a blue cloth have made
a paisley pattern

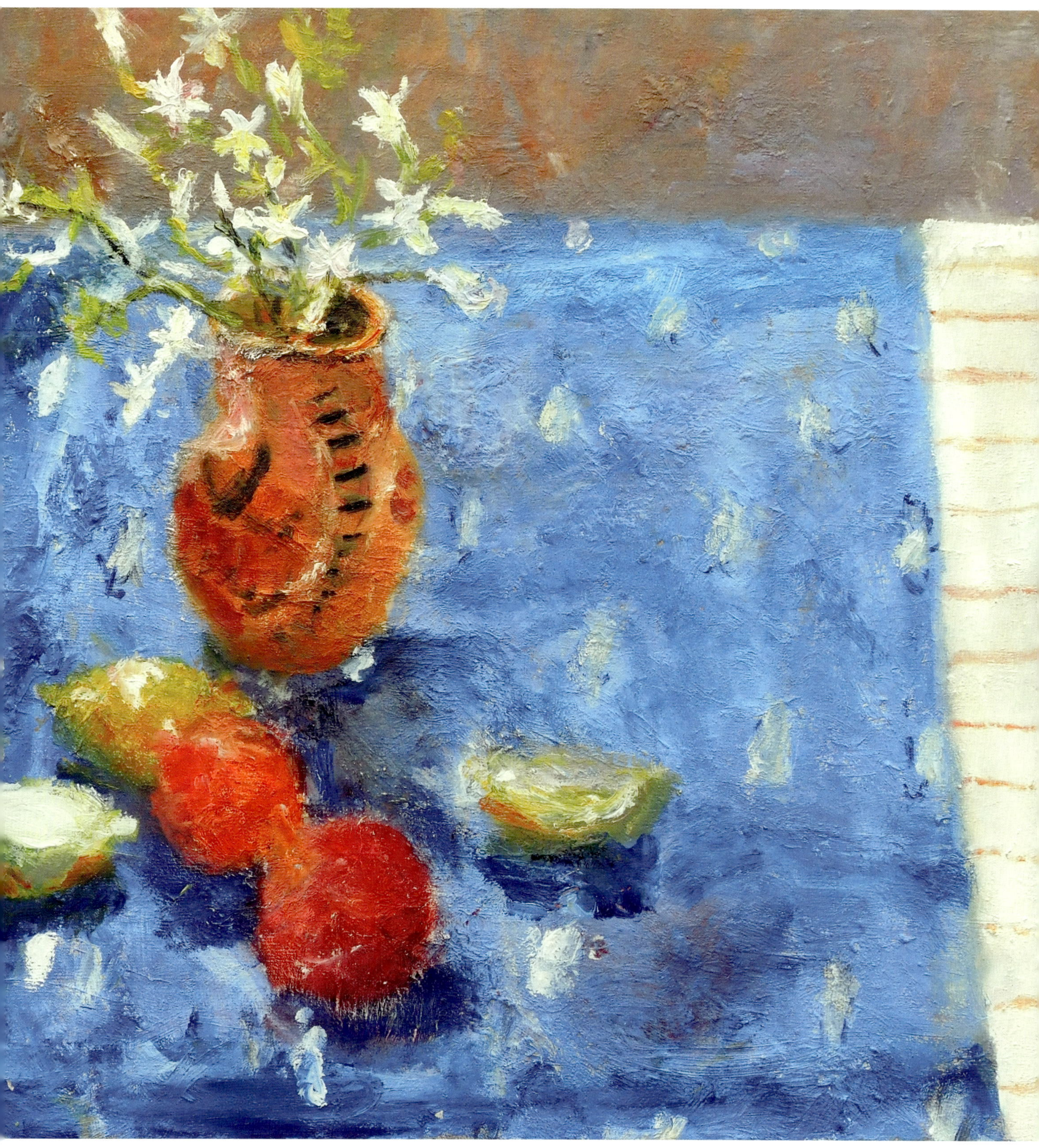

Jasmine and Blue · 2022 · oil on canvas · 60 x 60 cm

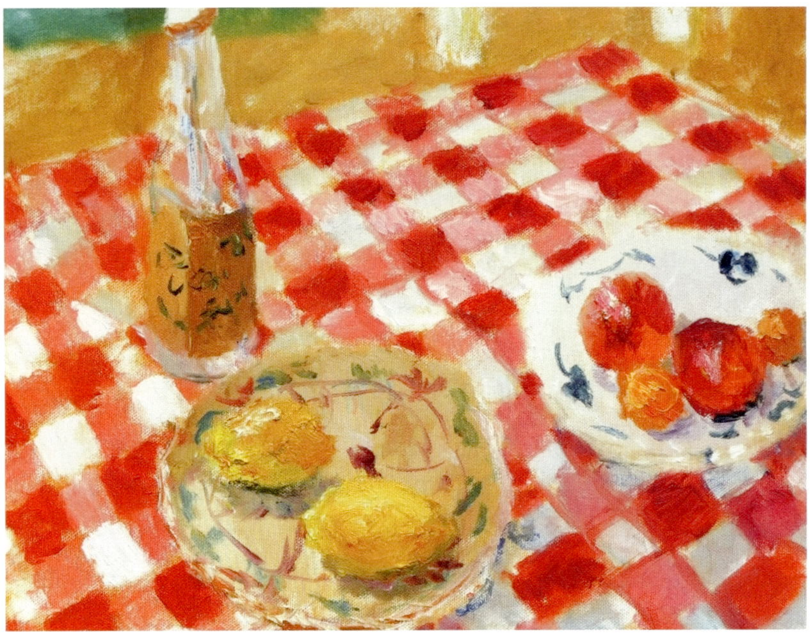

The Red and White Gingham Cloth and Olive Oil · 2022 · oil on canvas · 30.5 x 40.5 cm

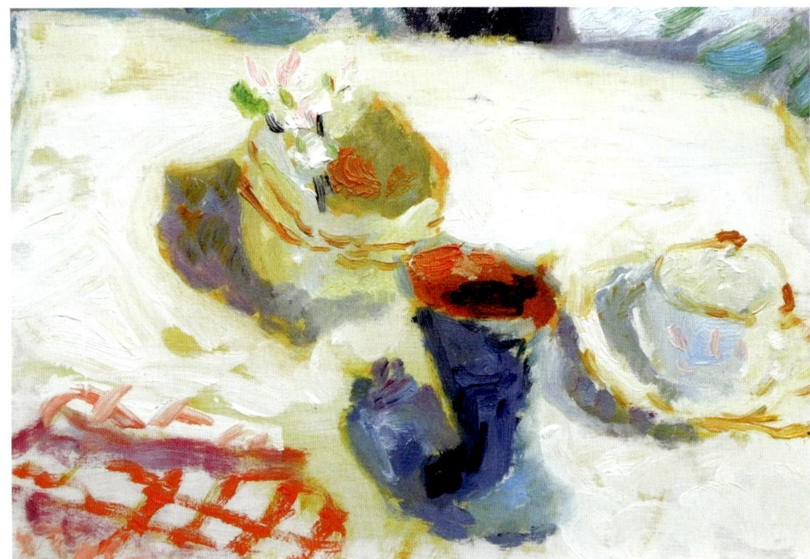

Electric Light and Small Blue Vase · 2022 · oil on board · 20 x 30.5 cm

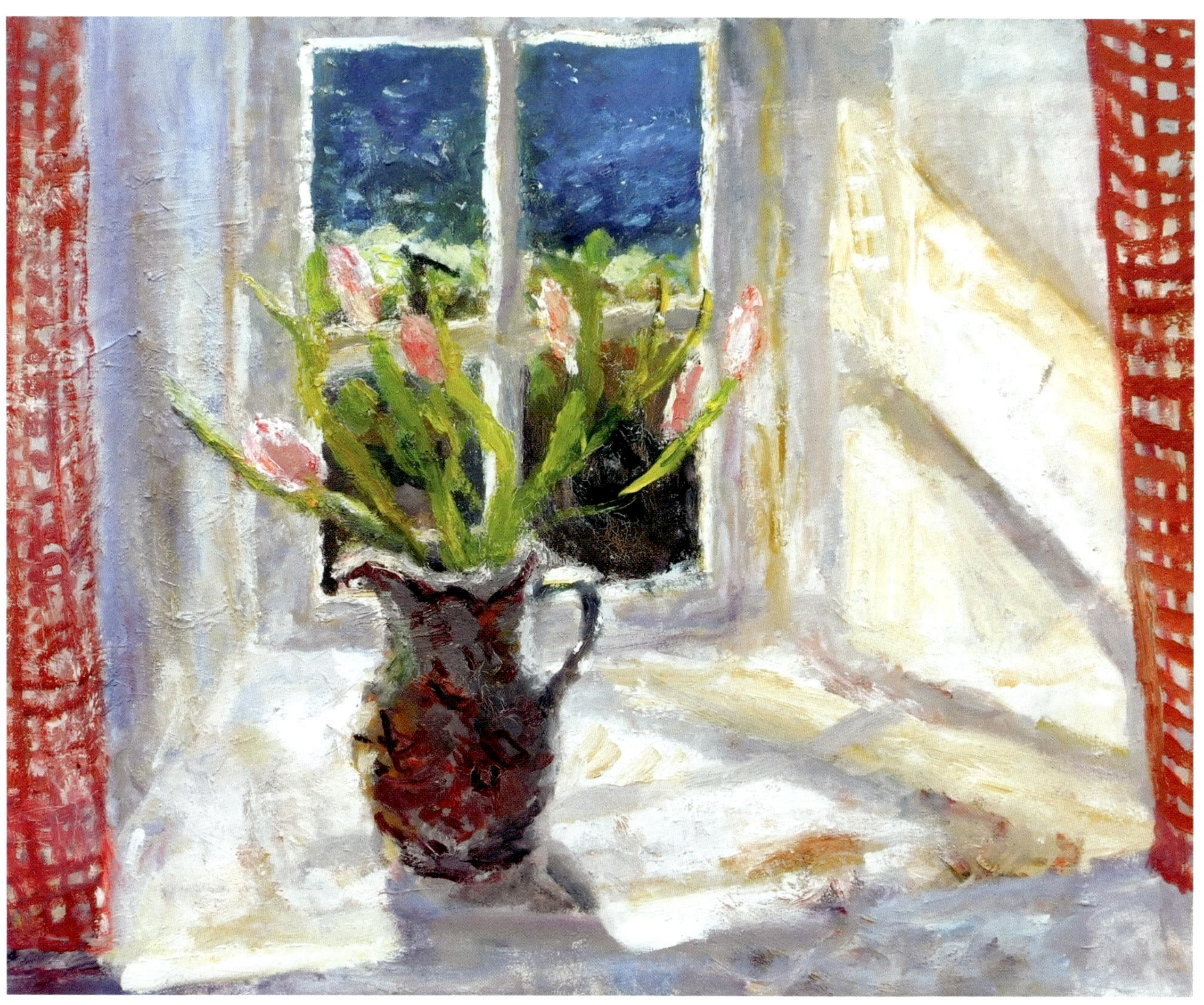

Seaward Window and Gingham Curtains · 2022–3 · oil on canvas · 61 x 76 cm

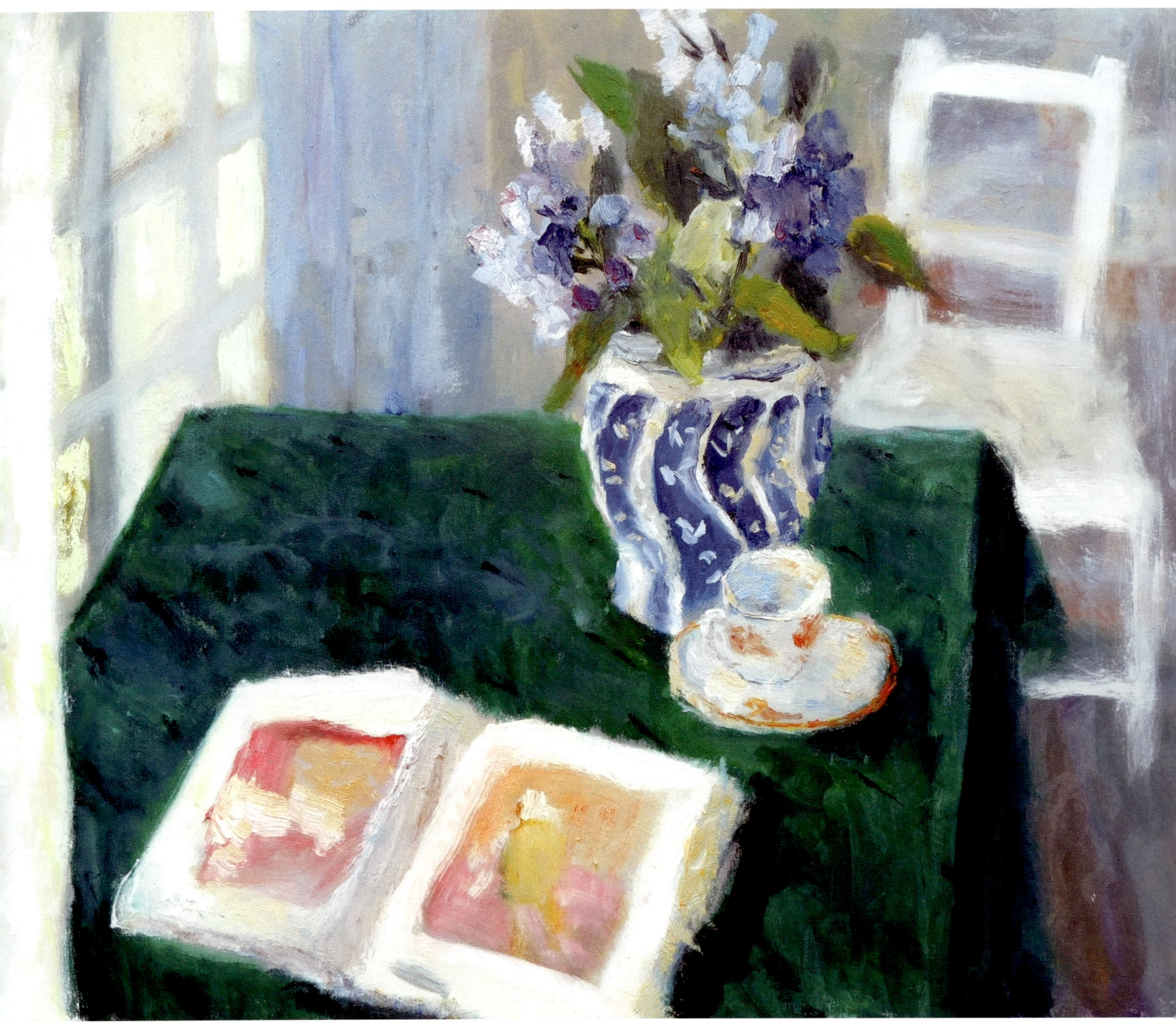

Emerald Green and Blues · 2022 · oil on canvas · 61 x 76 cm

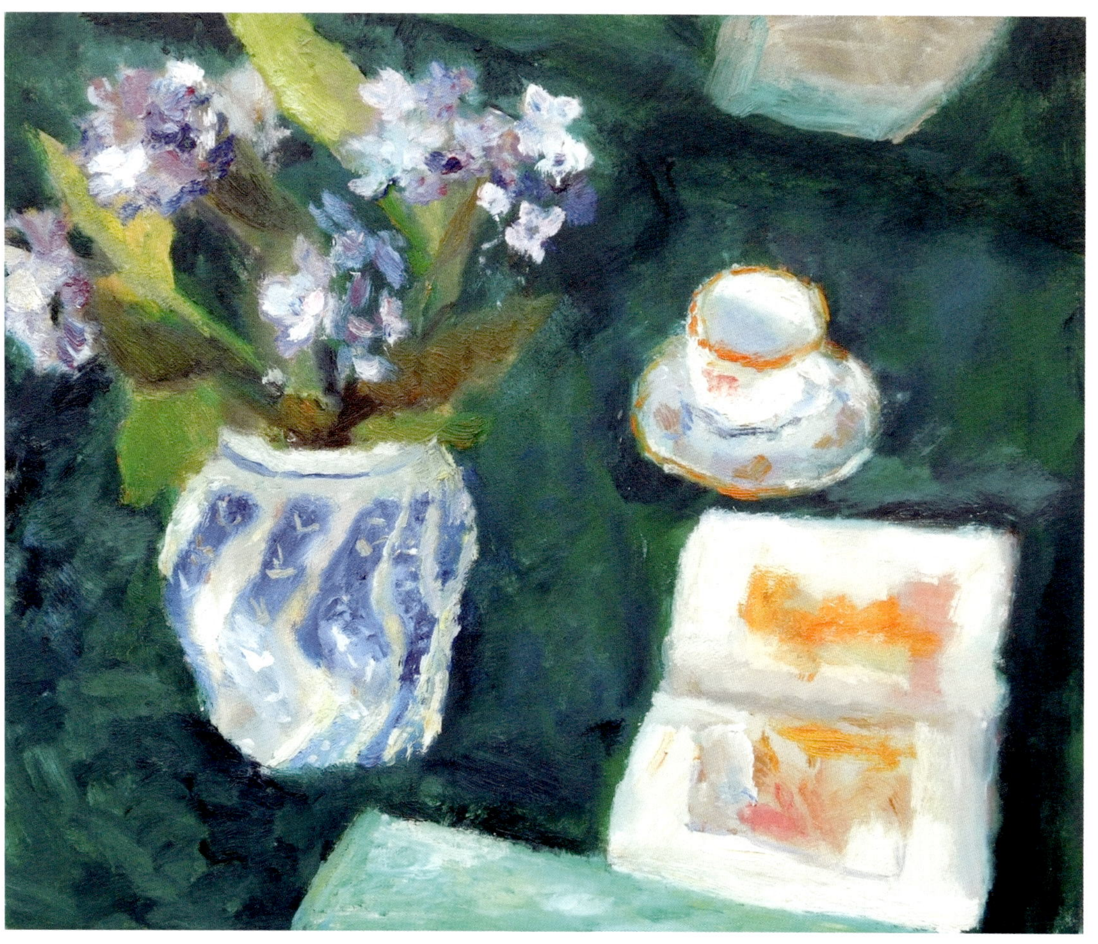

The Open Book on an Emerald Green Cloth · 2022 · oil on canvas · 50 x 60 cm

primrose light

did you walk
down that deep green lane
to Prussia Cove
in early sunlight
to pick pink-stemmed
primroses
(still lit
in their blue jug)

     *

the Jesuit priest-poet
talked of the *instress*
of primroses
I like his painterly image
the strong swell
given by the deeper
yellow middle

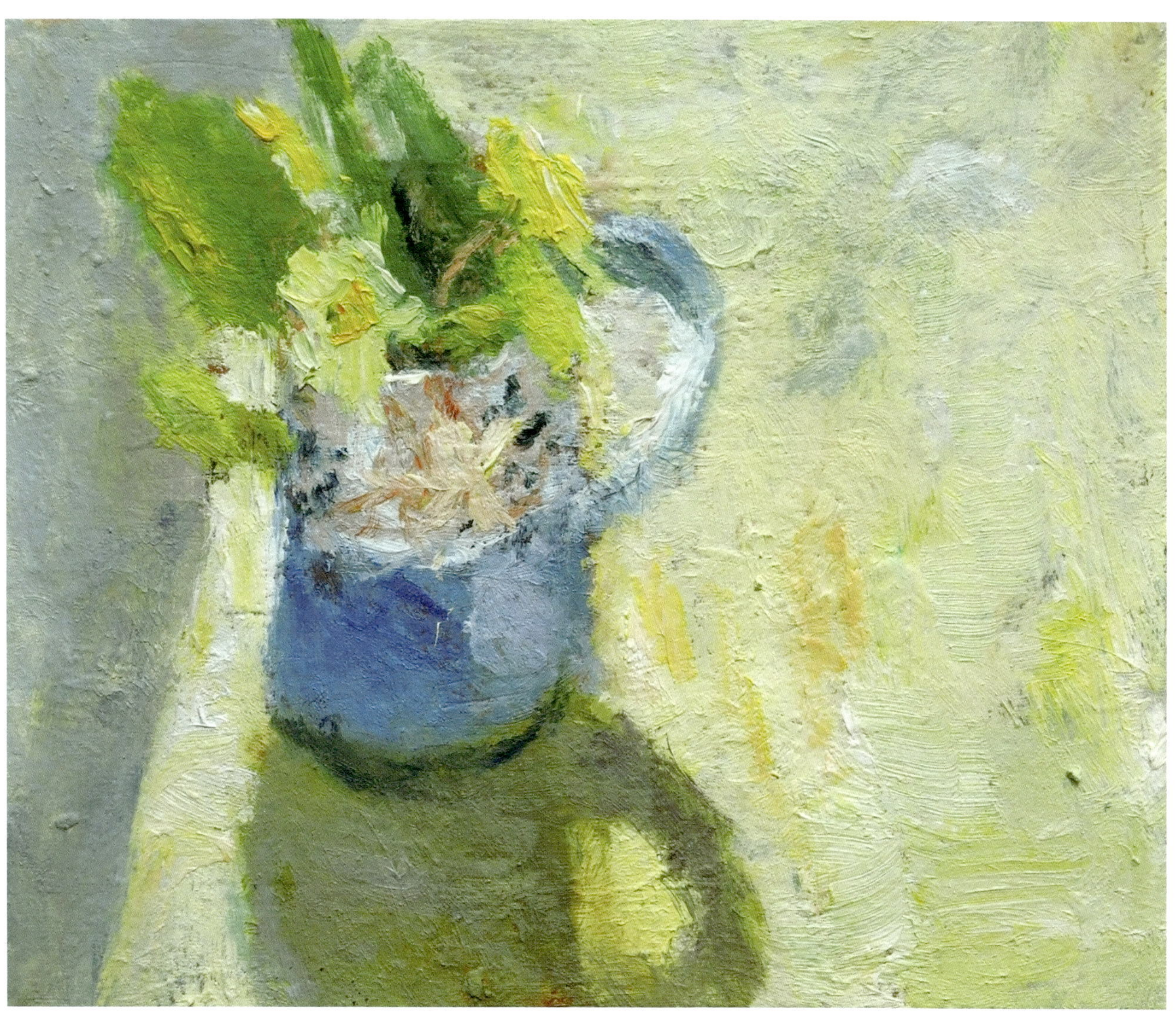

Primrose Arrival · 2022 · oil on canvas · 25.5 x 30.5 cm

Three views of the studio

Yours,
a sunny room at Polgrean
faded shutters blue-
green, jugs, tables,
flowers from your wild garden,
small still lives

on the walls your paintings
invite me to a place
more real
than this room
only your easel and brushes
remind me where I am

                    *

When Matisse travelled
to the south of France
he filled his suitcase
not with clothes
but textiles –
for a month or so
a hotel room becomes
his studio

                    *

Bonnard is mixing lemony-
yellow
because there is only
mimosa
this moment
passing
the joyous sadness of that

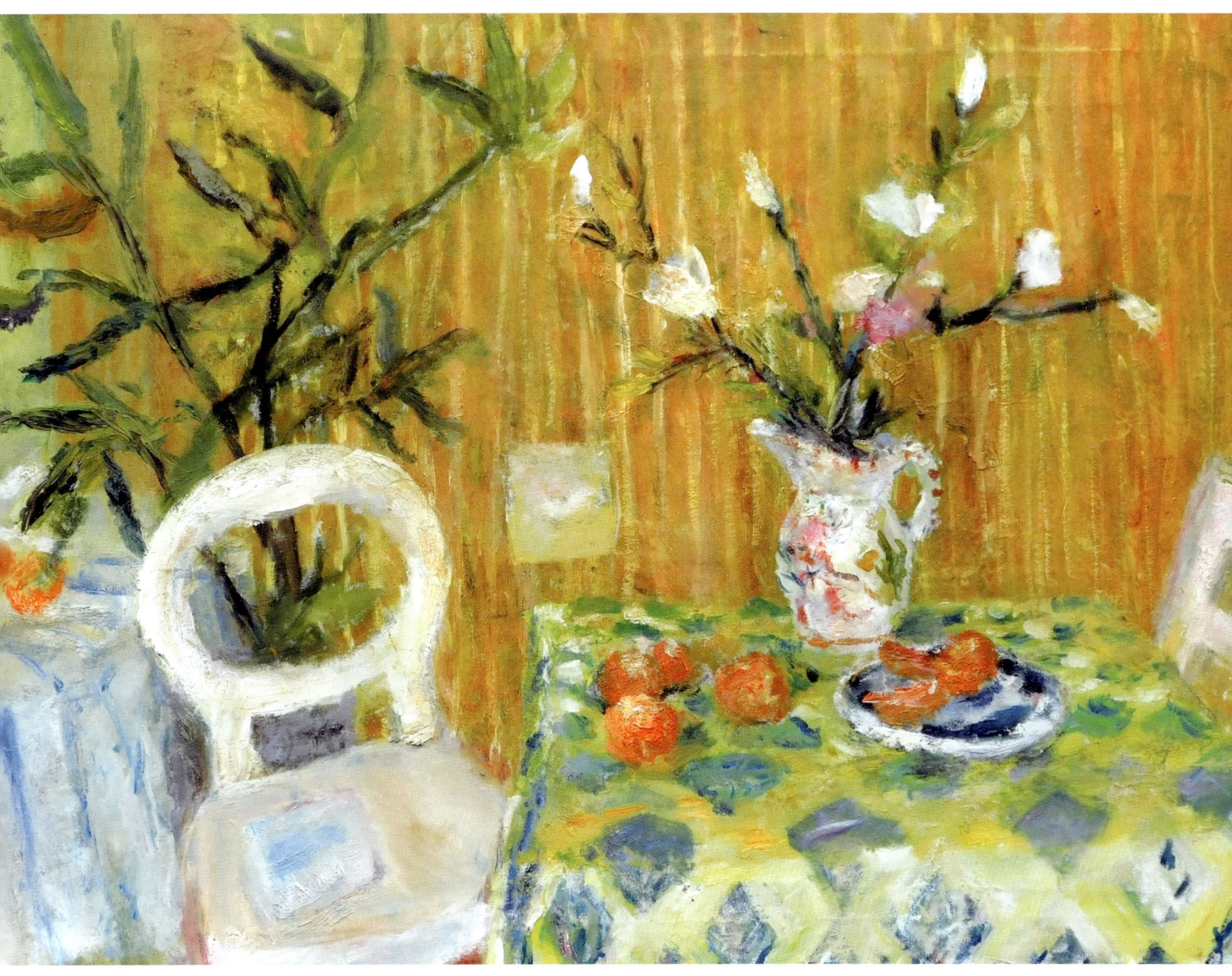

Matisse Day · 2022 · oil on canvas · 66.5 x 91.5 cm

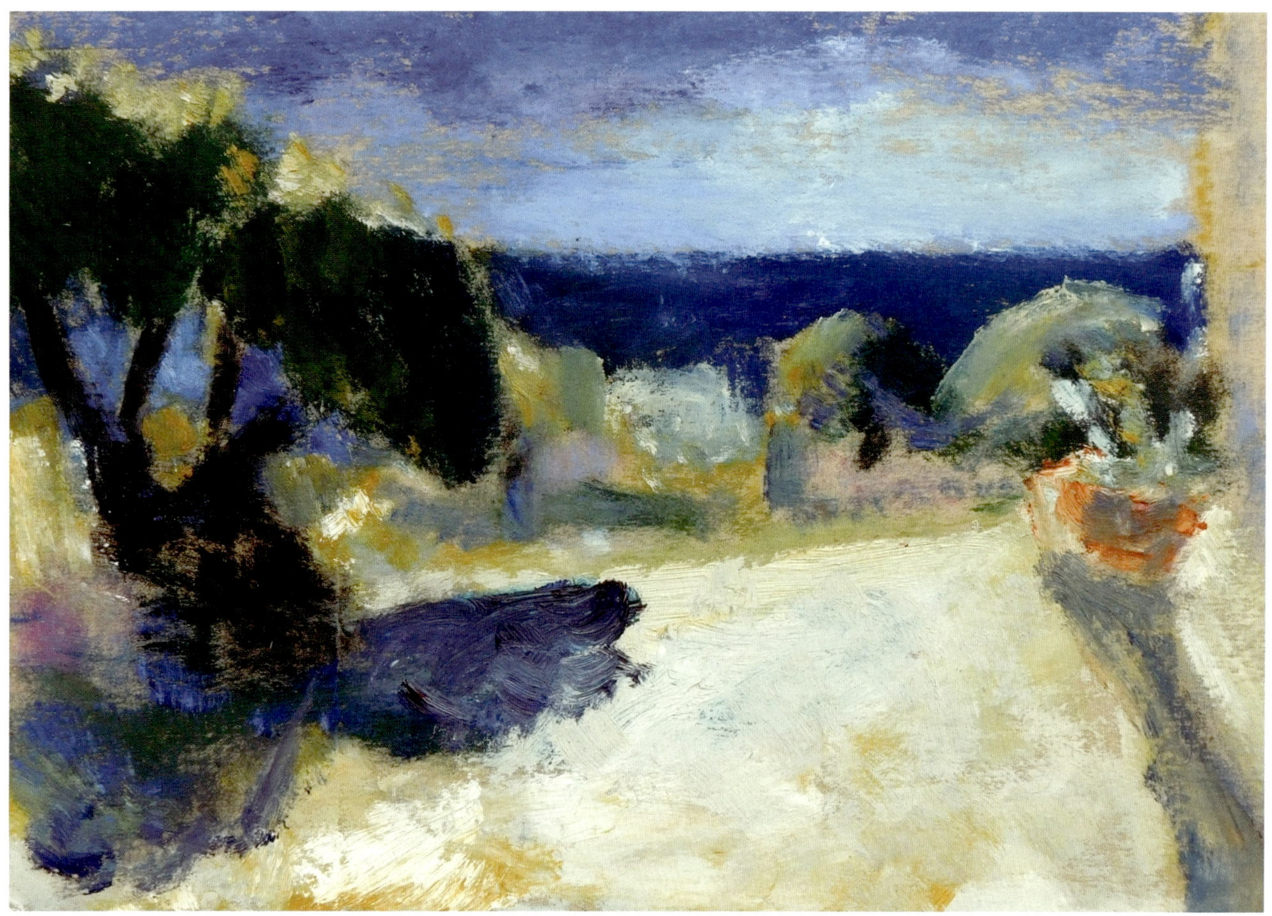

Summer Shadows, by the Sea · 2022 · oil on board · 21.5 x 31 cm

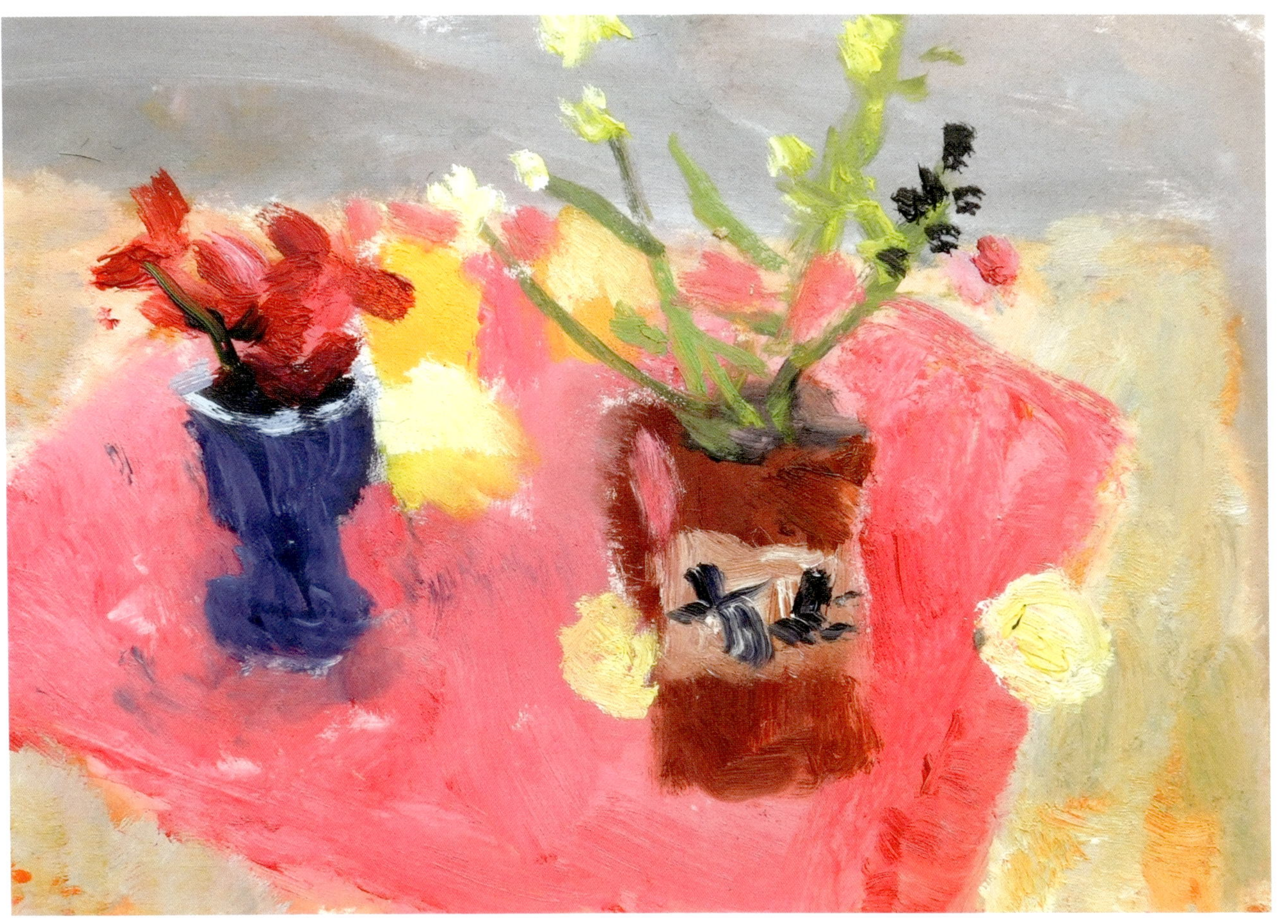

Pinks and Reds · 2022 · oil on board · 20 x 30 cm

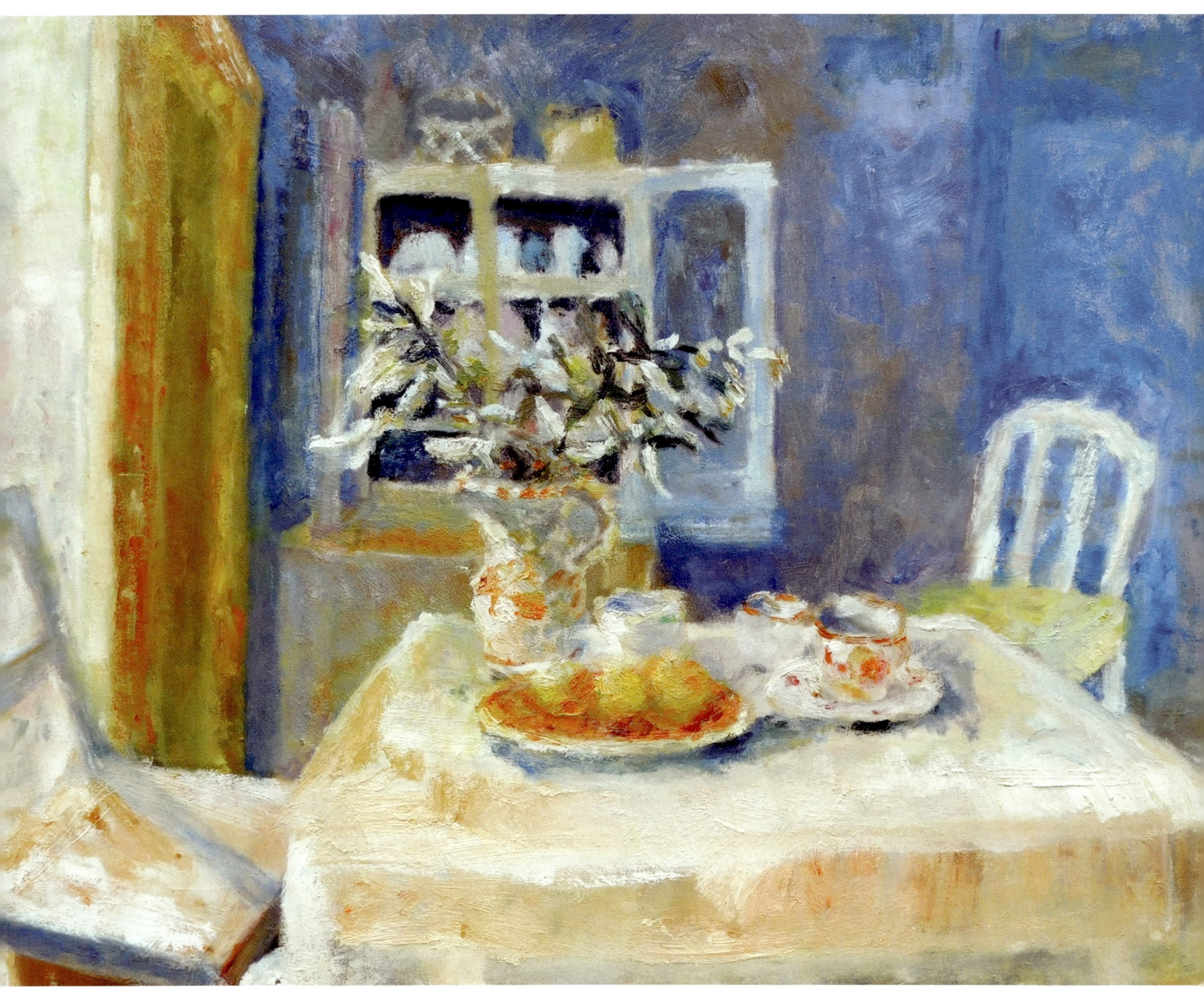

Early Sun in the Summer · 2022–3 · oil on canvas · 76 x 100 cm

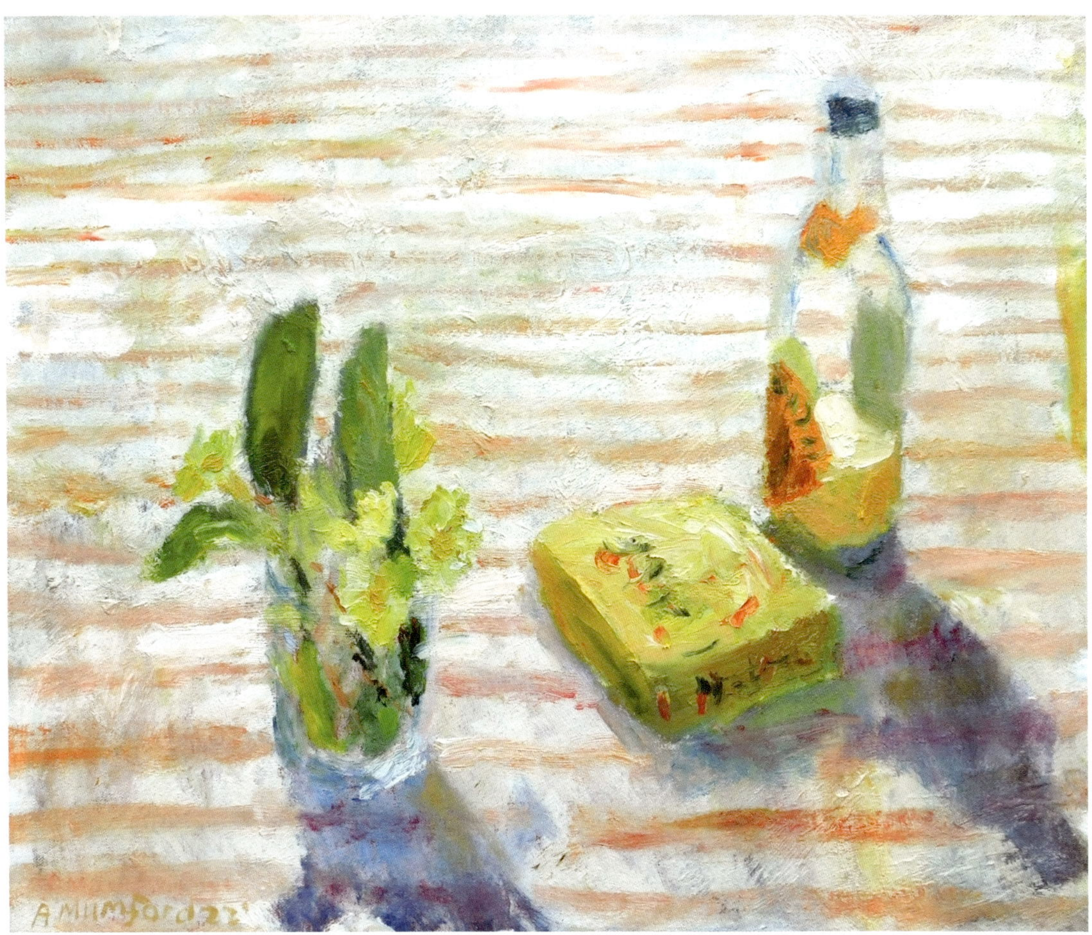

Fizzy Pop · 2022 · oil on canvas · 50 x 60 cm

painting light

here, sunlight falls
from a window
makes a white sail, makes another
window on the wall

apples deepen their reds
in the shadow of a terracotta jug

summer jasmine is
so white and starry
it might be night, might be
moonlight

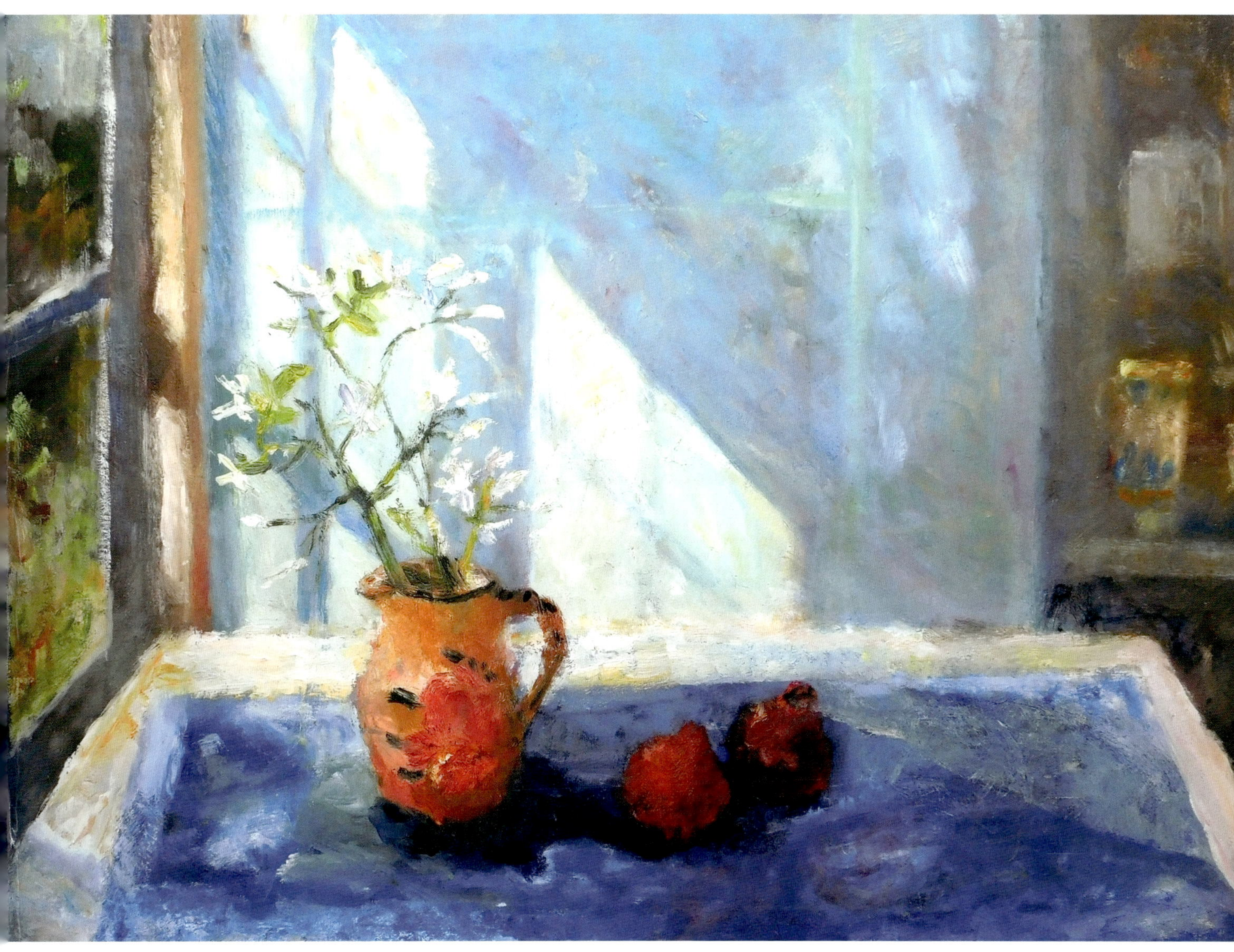

Summer Jasmine · 2021 · oil on canvas · 66.5 x 91.5 cm

the artists

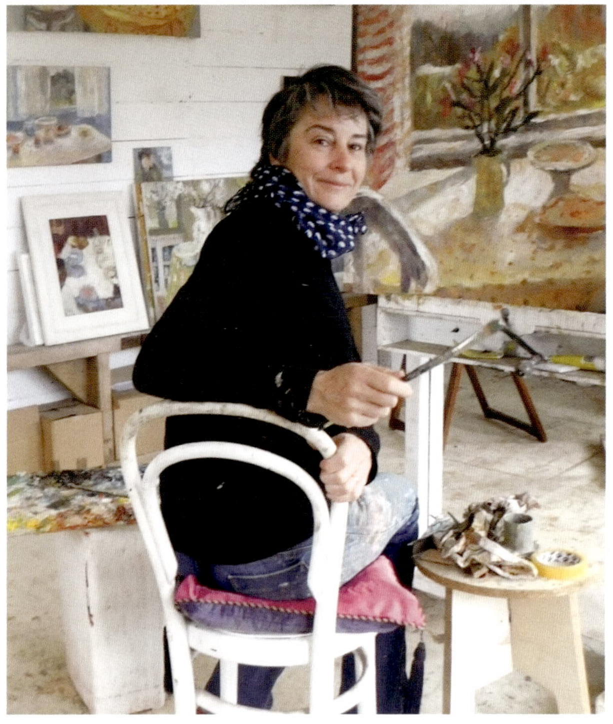

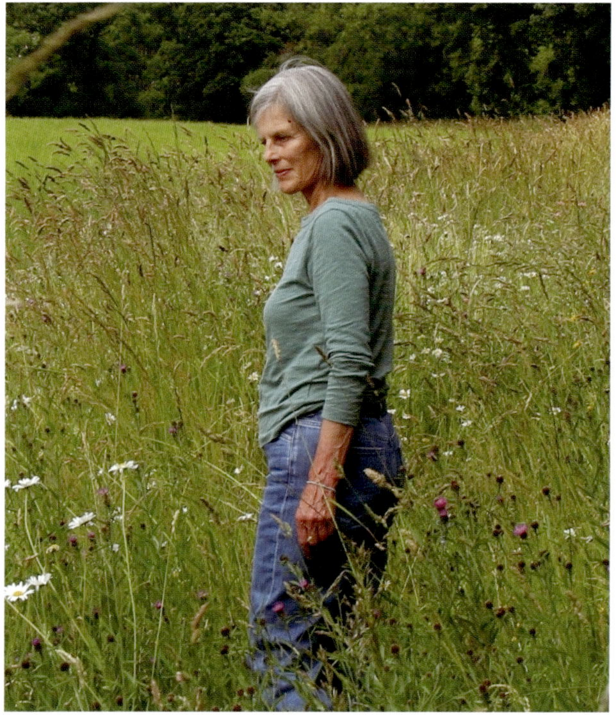

Alice Mumford was born in Bogota, Colombia. The family then moved to Norway. She went to Dartington Hall School in Devon in her teens, and then to Camberwell School of Art in 1984. She moved to Cornwall where her mother's family roots were. She has been exhibiting her paintings for over thirty years, with many sell-out solo shows. She has been teaching at the St Ives School of Painting for twenty-five years, and has made a series of short films for YouTube about ideas in painting. She was elected an RWA in 2010. She published *Colour from Coast to Coast* with Sansom & Company in 2015.

Sue Leigh worked for Faber for some years before moving to rural Oxfordshire. Her first book *Chosen Hill* (now reprinting) was described by the *TLS* as 'an intelligent and considered collection that pays homage to the act of paying attention'. This was followed by *Her Orchards* in 2021. A pamphlet 'Chalk' (printed by letterpress) was published in 2022. She teaches at Oxford University's Department for Continuing Education and runs her own poetry courses. She is working on a third book.

*

Kelly Grovier (foreword) is a poet and feature writer for BBC Culture. He is the author of ten books, including *The Art of Colour: The History of Art in 39 Pigments* (2023).